The Metaphysics of Experience

The Metaphysics of Experience

Truth, Enquiry and the Concept of Reality

A. C. Grayling

BLOOMSBURY ACADEMIC
LONDON · NEW YORK · OXFORD · NEW DELHI · SYDNEY

BLOOMSBURY ACADEMIC
Bloomsbury Publishing Plc, 50 Bedford Square, London, WC1B 3DP, UK
Bloomsbury Publishing Inc, 1359 Broadway, New York, NY 10018, USA
Bloomsbury Publishing Ireland, 29 Earlsfort Terrace, Dublin 2, D02 AY28, Ireland

BLOOMSBURY, BLOOMSBURY ACADEMIC and the Diana logo
are trademarks of Bloomsbury Publishing Plc

First published in Great Britain 2026

Contents

Preface vi

Acknowledgments xv

1 Introduction: The Argument 1

2 Natural Grammar and Ontology 11

3 Conceptual Schemes 31

4 Truth and Assertion 59

5 Metaphor 77

6 Reduction and Communicability 89

7 Enquiry and Modality 109

8 Reality and Deferral 137

References and Select Bibliography 162

Index 170

Preface

It is not the practice in technical philosophical work to begin on a personal note, but as the following is the precipitate of one strand of endeavour in a lifetime's involvement in philosophy, significant parts of which have been devoted to the pedagogy of the subject, public ethical and political concerns, and the attempt to convey philosophical ideas and styles of thought into public discourse, I wish to record the evolution and motivation of the argument here.

In the two decades after completing doctoral work at Oxford in 1982 (on epistemology, Kant and P. F. Strawson under the supervision of the latter and A. J. Ayer; part of the thesis contributed to *The Refutation of Scepticism* and later to *Scepticism and the Possibility of Knowledge*: publication details of these and the following titles mentioned in this Preface are appended to the Bibliography) I devoted attention to questions about metaphysical and semantic realism, meaning, truth, assertion and natural kinds, and to studies of Berkeley, Russell, Quine and Wittgenstein (the results are contained in a scholarly study *Berkeley: The Central Arguments* as a precursor both of positivism and phenomenalism, and in a series of papers eventually collected as *Truth, Meaning and Realism* and *Scepticism and the Possibility of Knowledge*, the former on the topics signalled in the title, the latter on the epistemologies of Russell, Quine and Wittgenstein. Short introductory books on Russell and Wittgenstein also resulted, in Oxford University Press's 'Past Masters' series). At the same time I contributed publications to philosophical pedagogy, represented by three successive editions of *An Introduction to Philosophical Logic* and (as editor) *Philosophy I: A Guide through the Subject* and *Philosophy II: Further through the Subject*. Further editorial roles with colleagues included *The Encyclopaedia of British Philosophy* (four volumes), *Humanism*, and *Metaphors and Analogies in Sciences and Humanities*.

For the next two decades my attention was devoted to applied ethics, political theory, the history of ideas and public and university education. Most of the books and essay collections on these subjects are addressed to a wider readership. The principal contributions in the history of ideas are *Towards the Light* and *The Age of Genius*, and in politics and public ethics are *Democracy and Its Crisis*, *The Good State*, *For the Good of the World*, *Discriminations*, *Who Owns the Moon* and *For the People*, the third and fifth examining the questionable robustness of international agreements on matters of global concern in light of threats posed by national economic self-interest and relativism, threatening as they do to prompt a tragedy of the commons, the others focusing on democracy and human rights.

The applied ethics and politics interests were prompted by public events – the climate crisis, Brexit, Trump, the rise of right-wing populism in many countries around the world among them. It seemed to me that those of us who have had the privilege and opportunity to study ideas have a responsibility to contribute, however modestly, perspectives on them to the general conversation.

Having essayed contributions to these matters I returned to the more technical questions of the preceding two decades, having continued to think about them and to develop the motivating ideas in them. The process of seeing these ideas in a more comprehensive light was potentiated by two things: writing *The History of Philosophy* brought the philosophical tradition's entire sweep of the evolution of these concerns into sharper focus, and writing *The Frontiers of Knowledge* – although a book for a more general readership on the state of knowledge in three significant domains (physics, history and neuropsychology) and the challenges to enquiry in them – triggered a *Gestalt* on the problem of knowledge addressed in my doctoral work and books on scepticism, and on the topics addressed in the papers on philosophical logic. Some of the earlier papers in this latter collection were first passes – among them some, in turn, that are unsatisfactory in retrospect – at trying to disentangle the questions which in the present volume have been addressed from a different angle and with a refreshed vocabulary. Fundamental problems in philosophy are perennially unfinished business; the deepening and sophistication of debate about aspects of them offers much progress, but the aim of articulating a perspective on them does not lend itself to remaining unfinished business to one absorbed by interest in them.

Hence the present book. In three respects it is the precipitate of developments of view throughout this long period of reflection on the questions at stake.

The first concerns the significance of seeing epistemological scepticism (the adjective 'epistemological' is required to distinguish challenges to justification for knowledge-claims from both religious scepticism and the healthy commitment to suspending judgment pending full examination in any field of enquiry, a desideratum of responsible research) is given renewed emphasis but in a different perspective, as powerfully identifying the challenges faced by beings of human scale and endowments as they seek knowledge. Views about conceptual-framework justifications for anchoring knowledge-claims satisfied me in the formulation I gave them for the empirical case; the development of them to a general theory of what is at work in all discourses is key to the finished case given here.

The second is a revised and developed view of the consequences of this for understanding the nature and role of assertion; understanding assertion is fundamentally important because of its intimate connection to concepts of truth, reference and the outcomes of methodologies of enquiry.

The third is the argument that the way much of the debate was earlier couched in terms of the 'realism-anti-realism' opposition (a hot topic at the time given the active contemporary influence of Dummett and interest in theories of meaning) was a distraction, not because it addressed the wrong topic – indeed, as argued in the Introduction below, it addressed the right topic: the epistemology of meaning – but because persistent misunderstandings about what was centrally at issue did not clarify but distorted it, and this informs the account here of the concept of reality, understanding which is the chief aim of the endeavour in these pages.

Such were the terms of the earlier framing of the debate that it was hard to persuade those committed to semantic realism that semantic anti-realism does not entail a rejection of metaphysical realism. Accordingly the question is here reframed as one about the way discourses project ontologies, thus showing that the relations between discourses and the domains over which they range are internal. By reversing the idea that perceptual discourse is the base case and that mimicry by other discourses of its grammar is a source of philosophical problems, I argue that a series of familiar philosophical problems are resolved thereby. The contention requires recognising that questions about the existence of referents in domains is an issue separate from the question of the epistemic relation of discourse to them. This in turn leads to the argument's conclusion: that the question of 'ultimate reality' has to be 'deferred' in the technical sense I give this notion.

Were I to draw attention to points that are arguably novel in this account, I would nominate these: that taking perceptual discourse as a putative base case misleads us, that '__is true' is a placeholder predicate, that a theory of assertion replaces theories of truth in a way that preserves the pretheoretical notion that truth (in the form of the more explicit properties of epistemic valuation for which it is a dummy) is substantive, that metaphor is irreducible in the discourse of perceptual experience and the 'is' of metaphor is its own form of copula, that the distinction between the placeholder truth predicate and its more precise substituends explains the contrast between validity and soundness, that 'actual' is a key modality, that epistemological scepticism identifies the challenges that enquiry must meet in a richer way than standardly recognised, that reductive exercises – in assuming that the question of ultimate reality is non-deferrable – generate problems as often as they illuminate them, that the concepts of 'actual' and 'real' are different, and that 'social reality' is as 'actual' as physical reality, that the discourse of perceptual experience is irreducibly internally inconsistent though for good practical reasons, and that the question of explicating the concepts of fundamental science in classical terms is at best only heuristically achievable because of this fact. In the course of substantiating these claims defences are given of a descriptive theory of reference and the ontological significance of natural language grammar.

There is doubtless much in these points that philosophical colleagues will dispute. But even if that is all these points achieve, it will be something from which we in our collaborative enterprise can benefit. On the other hand if the argument persuades, it has a chance of rerouting some of the more traditional preoccuptions of our endeavour away from dead-ends.

The strategy adopted in the following pages needs to be made clear from the outset. In the three or four decades preceding the writing of these words the volume of philosophical publications on the topics addressed here, and the degree of technicality involved, have both increased dramatically. It makes writing about these topics a daunting prospect, because in the standard case of current philosophical practice the ideal would be a full engagement with the literature on them. One driver to ever-narrower specialism in sub-domains of philosophy is precisely this anxiety, because it gives effect to the natural desire to be armed against the unforgiving ferocity of criticism – philosophy is a landscape in which fully armed intellectual security guards quite rightly lurk – by barricading oneself within a fortress of footnotes and references, thus among other things pre-empting accusations of ignorance regarding this or that view impinging on the suggestions being advanced. Severe criticism is a good thing, and there are those who think its withering effect in preventing some from venturing suggestions at all is an equally good thing (along the lines of 'everyone has a book in him and that's where it should stay'). But in my view it is even better to risk venturing a view which – although the chances of any view in philosophy commanding universal agreement are small – might spark further useful thoughts, or throw light on aspects of the vexingly persistent problems that philosophy wrestles with.

Therefore, in light of the extent and depth of the literature, service to the aim here requires that I assume antecedent familiarity with the debates in order to pass through – more accurately, navigate – them in order to pick out the points required for emphasis. Exegesis and discussion of the literature is not the aim; identifying a path through the debates they involve is the aim. An argument of this kind is like a jigsaw puzzle; the picture is only fully seen when all the pieces are in place. And the picture is a view of Monte Sainte-Victoire not an Anatomy Lesson; in the gallery of philosophical explorations there is wall-space for both.[1] I ask the reader to recognise this strategy from the outset.[2]

For one important thing, there will appear to be commitment to theses which turn out, once the key idea of *deferral* introduced and motivated in the final section is to hand, not to be what they seem. Given this, it might be thought that the notion should be introduced at the outset and its consequences for discourse ontology, reference, truth, enquiry and the other topics discussed, explained in its light. But in the process of organising the argument it transpired that explicating deferral itself rests on claims made about how these concepts are to be understood. Some of these claims are individually independent of the deferral thesis, but the deferral thesis rests on all of them collectively; hence the order of development.

Again as to the enormous quantity of literature and the entangling weeds of exegesis and criticism that engagement with it involves: here one is minded to quote R. G. Collingwood in his Preface to *Speculum Mentis*, his own attempt to navigate a route through the Himalayan passes of philosophical debate:

> There is hardly any philosopher whom I have read from whom I am not conscious of having learned something; and indeed one learns what one has it in one to learn, not what one's teachers have it in

---

[1] The references are, with due diffidence, to Cezanne and Rembrandt respectively.

[2] Take a volume of Hume in hand and ask: where are the footnote references to Descartes, Malebranche, Locke and Berkeley? Where is his discussion of their views, with agreement or refutation? In pursuing the aim of his argument he attended to his argument, not – as we now standardly do – to what he borrows or impugns in making it. But in line with Collingwood's point, shortly referenced, I think it is nevertheless pointful to acknowledge points of contact and difference in respect – in both senses of this term – to the rich literature clustered round these issues; and do so.

them to teach … On the other hand, to write a commentary without consulting previous commentaries would argue not scholarship but ignorance, not sincerity but frivolity. And *by greatly adding to the bulk of this volume I could easily have pointed out the affinities of my position with that of eminent writers past and present*, and so, perhaps, have recommended it to readers who rightly shrink from any philosophy advertised as new. *If I have consistently refrained from doing this it is only because I want my position to stand on its merits rather than on names of great men cited as witnesses for its defence.* But if the reader feels that my thesis reminds him of things that other people have said, I shall not be disappointed: on the contrary …(emphases mine).[3]

Collingwood goes on to say that he regards the argument in his book as his best effort to restate 'the essence of every great philosopher's teaching'. That is not the claim here, though an analogous one can be made: that much of the debate on the topics here discussed has resembled the enterprise of blind men patting an elephant, each describing the entire animal from that part of it – trunk, flank, leg – on which he happens to have his hands, one therefore saying an elephant is a long flexible tube (the trunk man), another that it is a broad flat expanse (the flank man), and so forth. Accordingly one might venture to claim to be trying to see the creature whole – and that is a venturesome claim enough.

Profiting from Collingwood's remarks as quoted, my strategy as regards the literature on the topics discussed here is to reference, in the standard way, thinkers and their texts when explicitly quoting, agreeing, using or disagreeing, but to make a more general acknowledgement when something kin is in the offing – indeed, to

---

[3] R. G. Collingwood, *Speculum Mentis* (Oxford University Press 1924).

employ the very phrase 'in the offing' to show that I am conscious that a view I offer is cognate to, reminiscent of, has some parallels with, or stands in contrast or opposition to, related views. Accordingly, in speaking of the discourse-relativity of ontologies I might footnote thus: 'In the offing, Carnap on theory-relativity of existence, Quine on quantifying-over'; talking of deflationary accounts of truth, 'In the offing, Ramsey, Strawson, Horwich', etc. In this way I hope to honour the participants in the debate and acknowledge the debts – however indirect, and both positive and negative – I owe them, while attempting my own twist of the kaleidoscope on the matters here discussed.

The footnotes frequently provide significant commentary on the discussion in the main text, so the asides, comments and clarifications there are indispensable as support for the suggestions offered in the main text.

Acknowledgments

This book has been very long in gestation, and it is hard to single out a few from the many who have played a part, large or small, in the trajectory followed. Among numerous others there were: early on, Peter Strawson, Freddie Ayer, Michael Dummett, David Pears, John Mackie, Michael Wood, Bernard Harrison, Timothy Sprigge; among fellow students at Oxford there were Flint Schier, Josh Tonkel, Joe Palumbo, Michael Luntely; later there were Alex Orenstein, Gabrielle Taylor, Dan Dennett, Peter Singer, Petr Kotatko, Barry C. Smith, Marcus Giaquinto, Mark Sainsbury, Simon Blackburn, Hilary Putnam; audiences at the Graduate Centre, City University of New York, the Australian National University, the universities of St Andrews, Sydney, Edinburgh, Sussex, Glasgow, East Anglia, Melbourne, Durham, London, Oxford, Exeter, Wales, Hawaii, Tokyo, Chiba, the Institute of Philosophy of the Czech Academy of Sciences, the Chinese Academy of Social Sciences, and more; and not least of the 'more' the New College of the Humanities and Northeastern University. The phrases 'among others' and 'and more' indicate these as saliences in memory, and I apologise for omissions – not all of many speaking engagements at universities were to philosophy departments, for student and debating societies at these and numerous other places did not often involve addressing the content of the pages here. Contributions at conferences at these and other places are not included, although as

Secretary of the Aristotelian Society for a decade I heard much that osmosed. As an editor of philosophical books I had the privilege of stimulating encounter with yet many others. Along with those named, the living presence of thinkers from Parmenides to our day have to be included, the names of Aristotle, Hume and Kant standing out in significance.

It is pointful to note that these acknowledgments pertain only to the concerns of this book. 'Philosophy' in its broader historical connotation, addressing the problems of life and society, reaches well beyond the concerns of the narrow specialisms of academic analytic philosophy, within which the discussion of this present book lies. Were I to acknowledge the contributions and examples that have borne upon other endeavours made, they would range from Zeno of Citium, Epicurus, Cicero, Seneca and Epictetus, via Erasmus, Montaigne and William Hazlitt to Arthur Schopenhauer, John Stuart Mill and Bertrand Russell – not such an eclectic mix as might at first appear. And that is to leave out the great philosophers who appear under the labels 'poets', 'essayists', 'dramatists' and 'novelists' on the shelves of bookshops and libraries. The distance between the detailed concerns of analytic philosophy and the life-enriching contributions of those for whom praxis was as great if not greater a moment than gnosis is not as large as it appears – a claim worthy of demonstration, for another time.

§ 1

Introduction: The Argument

The suggestion in what follows is that if we pursue the implications of a certain way of understanding a fundamental feature of natural language use, we will see several significant philosophical topics in new light. These topics are reference, truth, assertion, the nature of enquiry, modality, and conceptions of reality itself. At first blush this might seem an ambitious list of targets, but – first – a moment's reflection reminds one that the topics are so intimately linked that a reset of views on any one of them has inevitable consequences for the others, and – second – in any case the outcome of the discussion will in fact be modest, particularly in connection with conceptions of reality, where the conclusion supported by the argument is that the concept of *ultimate* reality – a basal ontology which takes reductions from all other domains over which our discourses range and which is causally and explanatorily final in relation to them – has to be *deferred*, in a sense of 'deferral' to be introduced and explained as a technical concept (§8).

The supporting case for this suggestion argues that ontologies are projected by universal categories of natural language grammar for the domains over which discourses range, and that, as an essential feature of the discourses' pragmatics, the conceptual schemes thus framed are ad hoc for creatures of the scale and endowments of human beings – alternatively put: are configured for the convenience of such creatures – their ad hoc nature resulting in incommensurabilities and inconsistencies. But these are in general *useful* incommensurabilities and inconsistencies given the scale and endowments in question. Recognising this is highly consequential for understanding reference and the concepts of truth and assertion adaptively at work in discourses, and reveals the constraints under which enquiry into their domains works.

As a taster for the points just described: one outcome is a demonstration of why theories in fundamental physics (quantum theory and its future refinements and developments if these latter take the theory further into applications of such concepts as entanglement, superposition, uncertainty and wave-particle duality) cannot be interpreted in classical terms other than heuristically by means of analogy and metaphor, not because of anything putatively wrong with quantum theory but because the conceptual scheme of perceptual experience at the classical (ordinary, everyday) level is composed of the incommensurabilities and inconsistencies – together with irreducible use of metaphor – indulged for the organisation of experience at that level, rendering it such that the concepts of quantum theory can get at best only figurative purchase in its terms.[1] If this is right, the project of accounting for the realm of perceptual experience by means of a

---

[1]Decoherence is offered as an account of how quantum states can appear as classical states from the point of view of observation at the classical level. The questions this prompts include: Why is the classical level privileged? Why do we take it to be the test of what is real? (These are two different questions.) In any case, what does a classical state look like from a scale greater by many factors than the classical level? In what way is the *human* scale definitive of the classical as a whole – and is that all ranges of the classical, from mites to galaxies? For by transitivity, this makes the human scale the test of what is real at any scale. And although a claim to this effect could be true, it cannot be so regarded

reduction of its discourses to a scientific discourse – in the projected ideal, a unified such discourse – looks unrealisable. Mention of this is illustrative; this is not a discussion of interpretations of quantum theory, although as a consequence of the argument here this claim is significant for understanding the implications of natural language's projection of ontologies in general.

As a preliminary defence against the scepticism that the foregoing might provoke, note that the state of cognitive neuroscience at time of writing represents a catching-up with what Parmenides, Plato, Spinoza, Berkeley, Hume, Kant and assorted idealists and phenomenalists each in their own way have long argued: that the world of everyday perceptual experience is a virtual reality, and that candidates for '*real* reality', whatever they are, are something other. Antirealists about mathematical entities and moral properties take a yet more emphatic view, that there is no 'real reality' in the case at all. The observations of cognitive neuroscience at very least suggest the pertinence of a reassessment of the conceptual scheme of everyday perceptual experience. It is upon undertaking this in the light of the 'virtual reality' point that one registers the ad hoc nature of the scheme, and the implications of this for philosophical understanding of the key notions of reference, truth and the others – and of how these thoughts relate to other discourses and their domains.

---

without argument and evidence in support. On another tack: is the incommensurability of quantum and classical physics established by the undecidability of the spectral gap; see 'The Undecidability of the Spectral Gap' by T. S. Cubitt et al., *Forum of Mathematics, Pi* 10 (2022): 2015: 'Even a perfect, complete description of the microscopic interactions between a material's particles is not always enough to deduce its macroscopic properties'. In this case ontological irreducibility is in the material mode what incommensurability of discourses is in the linguistic mode, making descriptions of levels of phenomenal organisation in which one manifests emergent properties undeducible from another – where the latter is assumed to be more basic – a classic manifestation of incommensurability.

In naming this book *The Metaphysics of Experience* I have chosen a deliberately hybrid title, hybrid because whereas reference to metaphysics implies questions about ontology (and therefore the concepts of existence and reality), 'experience' evokes concerns in epistemology and the philosophy of mind. And indeed the title could as well be *The Metaphysics of Epistemology* in light of the book's argument, which is that our discourses are ways of knowing that project (posit, imply, accroach: but 'project', verb, is the *mot juste*) an ontology for the domains over which they range, and that the various ways of representing this – for example by saying that 'linguistic capacity consists in knowing meanings' and that 'experience at the human scale in the universe is organised by the way we construct meanings' – throw much light on the nature of the fundamental problem in metaphysics: viz. knowing the nature of ultimate reality.

One aspect of the argument here, already mentioned in part, is that what might be called 'ontological anxiety', viz. the problem of identifying '*real* reality', has – although a perennial since the pre-Socratics – acquired renewed intensity as a result of the marked successes of fundamental physics and cognitive neuropsychology, both which undermine once and for all the naïve pretheoretical assumption which, despite being so, has always been a determining factor in thinking about reality, indeed serving as reality's touchstone; namely, the belief that the medium-sized dry-goods world over which ordinary perceptual experience ranges provides us with the paradigm of what is real – the position, tacitly presupposed as the test case even when theoretically disowned, known as 'naïve realism'. Despite the frequently-issued challenge to this conception from Parmenides to the phenomenalists, this view has not only been the metaphysics of 'the man in the street' but – in at very least the form of the test-case presupposition – of most philosophers and scientists, so compellingly that debates about scepticism in epistemology have focused on defending, against sceptical challenge, either the belief in the conception itself or at least its intelligibility, while the apparent incompatibility of fundamental science's depiction of the quantum realm with classical depictions of reality is seen as a peculiarly vexing dilemma – recall the fundamental point at issue between Einstein and Bohr over the ontology of quantum theory.[2]

Indeed it is remarkable (and made strikingly obvious by accounts of the debates and anxieties of quantum theory's founders, who were philosophically as well as scientifically sophisticated), how much hold the dry-goods conception had – and still has: consider van Fraasen's discussion of the view that truth-values can be assigned only to statements about 'observables', these being what can be detected by means of the human senses and presumably their extensions by means of telescopes, microscopes and other instruments, and that evaluation of all other claims in science turns instead on their 'empirical adequacy', tested by success in saving the phenomena.[3] Arthur Fine's invocation of a 'Natural Ontological Attitude' extends to the referents of terms in predictively successful science the presuppositions of naïve realism about the status of entities encountered in perceptual experience – a view that in effect says, by analogy with the latter case, 'The theory in which the terms are couched works; why not just say or accept that their referents exist'.[4] When dispute is joined on the question of realism in the

---

[2]E.g. Max Jammer, *The Philosophy of Quantum Mechanics* (Wiley 1974).

[3]Bas van Fraasen, *The Scientific Image* (Clarendon Press 1980) 11–19. See such responses as e.g. Paul Churchland, 'The Ontological Status of Observables' in Churchland and Hooker (eds.) *Images of Science* (Chicago University Press 1985).

[4]Arthur Fine, 'The Natural Ontological Attitude' in Janet Kourany, *Scientific Knowledge*, 2nd edn. (Cengage Learning 1997) 97–102. See also his 'And Not Anti-Realism Either' ibid., 365–68.

philosophy of science between those who take the truth of theories to be the chief issue, and those who regard the existence of entities to be the chief issue, where the former seeks an account that dispenses with commitment to the latter (otherwise there is no inconsistency between the views), the point of departure for understanding 'exists' and 'real' is their pretheoretical meanings in the 'natural ontological' case. Were that not so, the disputants would be talking past each other.

But quantum theory and the findings of cognitive psychology have demonstrated the pertinence of – indeed, it would be more accurate to say, have caught up with the insights in – arguments in the philosophical tradition from as early as Parmenides variously to the effect that *reality* is not the way it *appears* to beings of the dimensions and endowments of humans. For this reason the question of 'the ultimate nature of reality' remains not only as philosophically pressing as ever, but arguably more so because any lingering assumptions about what has long served as the standard exemplification of it is no longer sustainable.

And this is so despite the fact that 'the man in the street' – let us say: *l'homme moyen instruit* – probably now shifts the touchstone of reality from medium-sized dry goods to their constituents, so far as he understands them: the atomic particles or quantum fields which compose them. Making the occasional reference (it makes no difference to practice whatever) to a chair's being mostly empty space (etc.) is a nod in that direction. But dry goods as 'real things', even though composed of tiny bits, remain as real as ever they were.

In one good sense this is of course as it should be, because no-one sane can deny – in that good sense – the reality of chairs and tables. The point is that chairs and tables are not examples of what is *ultimately* real. And the idea that quarks and leptons, or fields or strings, constitute the *ultimate* reality, is – although quarks and leptons are actual enough (hadrons composed of the former can be smashed together and the debris informatively investigated, as at CERN's Large Hadron Collider) – also moot, metaphysically.

If the discussion in the pages here achieves its aim, it will focus a shift in the nature of the question to be asked, from 'What is real?' to 'Which discourse's ontology should be privileged as the touchstone ontology, even if it is not the ontology to which all others can be remainderlessly reduced – and why?' But certain crucial points require comment before the import of this question, innocuous as it seems in itself, is clear, and to these, and the answer to the question they suggest, this book is devoted.

The family of topics at issue here was debated, in this writer's philosophical juvenescence, in terms of the 'realism-anti-realism' opposition.[5] But – to repeat the claim made in the Preface above – this way of approaching things looks now like a distraction, not because it addressed the wrong topic, for indeed it addressed the right topic: viz. the epistemology of meaning, but because persistent misunderstandings about what was really at issue in the debate did not clarify but distorted it. These misunderstandings rested on the view held by those on the realist side of the conversation that semantic anti-realism implies rejection of metaphysical realism. Repeated attempts to show that this is not so, and therefore to identify the correct interpretation of what semantic anti-realism involved, gained little traction.[6] In the argument of the present book the question is reframed to focus on the way discourses project ontologies, thus showing that the relations between discourses and the domains over

---

[5] E.g. M. Dummett, *Philosophy of Language* (Polity 2013); A. C. Grayling, 'Understanding Realism' and 'How Not to Be Realistic' in *Truth, Meaning and Realism* (Continuum 2007).
[6] Grayling, *Truth, Meaning and Realism* 2007.

which they range are *internal* ones in both the directions *discourse to domain* and *domain to discourse*. Semantic realism was committed to the view that the relations are hybrid – *internal* in the direction *domain to discourse* because mental contents cannot be individuated without essential reference to what lies outside the head, but *external* in the direction *discourse to domain* because what lies outside the head is 'independent' (here they meant 'existentially independent') of mental contents intending them. My claim then, and point now, is that the *existence* of domains and what they contain is an issue *separate* from the question of the epistemic relation of discourse (thought and talk) to them – *importantly* separate: for much follows from holding apart the tasks of explaining each.

This recognition, in its turn, provides a way of thinking about the implications for the key metaphysical question, namely, the nature of *ultimate* reality, where ultimacy consists in causal and explanatory reductive finality. In a technical sense to be given to the notion I introduce here of 'deferral' (§8), the argument is that the question, 'Which ontology is fundamental?' (alternatively, 'Which discourse is privileged metaphysically and epistemologically because irreducibly?') has to be *deferred* – meaning conceptually (not temporally; for at the same time this is not a claim that we will never, on separate grounds, be in principle incapable of doing so). An informal way of putting this is to say: a commitment to the existence of a determinate reality independent of knowledge or experience of it is inescapable, and can be shown to be so (or at least: the claim that it is so can be cogently motivated), as is commitment to that reality's being causally connected to experience of it; but that the resources of the conceptual schemes which organise the ontologies of our discourses ('our' meaning human beings, given the human physical scale and cognitive endowments) do not privilege any of them as *the* one that is 'ultimate' in the sense of ontological ultimacy to be described here.

It will, or should if it is not already so in the foregoing, become clear that the argument here has nothing to do with the kind of views variously to the effect that nothing counts as 'external reality' but that there are '*only* discourses', still less that different discourses are equally valid (as in the relativist claim that there is nothing to choose between, on the one hand, stimulating rainfall by silver iodide seeding of clouds and, on the other hand, dancing round a totem pole[7]) – in short, this is not an essay in postmodernism, but a contribution to one of the most central and longstanding debates in philosophy: the debate about what there is, and how we do or at least can hope to know it. In the course of the argument to the concept of metaphysical deferral, considerations of natural language ontology, truth, reference, assertion and methodologies of enquiry need to be taken into consideration, and it is to these that the sequel is addressed.

---

[7] In the offing, Paul Feyerabend, *Against Method* (New Left Books 1975).

§ 2

Natural Grammar and Ontology[*]

A good place to start is to note that naïve realism about the spatio-temporal realm of concrete particulars and events involving

---

them – the realm over which ordinary perceptual experience ranges – is a natural corollary of the way human language works.[1]

Suppose, as it is plausible to do, that the first developments in the evolutionary history of language were mainly concerned with drawing the attention of others to features of a perceptual environment – almost certainly, at the outset, by ostensive definition of primitive referring expressions, continuing what were undoubtedly the prelinguistic means of directing companions' attention – together, soon enough, with ways of describing those expressions' referents in order to identify and individuate them, useful when referents were absent from the immediate perceptual environment. If this is how things linguistically began, we may take the grammar of this language to consist in expressions used to label things (objects and events), expressions used to describe their properties (the qualities and relations of things), and expressions used to indicate their behaviour (the modalities of activity involving the things). Prepositions, conjunctions and determiners would have developed as the communicative needs and capacities of the linguistic community grew, and with them tenses and moods as the importance increased of talking about the past, the future, active and passive conditions, and possible states of affairs elsewhere.

This is an outline taxonomy of basic grammatical features of natural language, minimalistically conceived; it is consistent with notions of 'universal grammar' but trades specifically on the intuitive idea of how language evolved *ab initio* (thus, a view about the acquisition of language) and leaves aside questions of innate structure and

---

[1]Throughout I employ the locution 'perceptual experience' rather than 'empirical experience' for the obvious reason that the latter has a more copious extension, including in its domain unobservables accessed by instrumental or theoretical means. Because the base case ontology from discourse about which, in the history of concepts, both scientific extensions and philosophical problems arise, is that of perceptual experience, this is the *phrase appropriée.*

the repertoire of linguistic theories that challenge Chomskean views. The plausibility of a primitive Baconian conception of underlying commonalities in language as a shared system of communication is assumed.[2]

In origin the basic categories of the primitive language just described are taken to apply to the perceptual environment of its speakers, and accordingly embodies their ontology. No doubt the ontology had or soon acquired a rich cultural gloss of meanings in which, as anthropology suggests, things were agents or inhabited by them, and possessed powers and properties beyond those encountered empirically in interaction with them. But at the base of the language lie denotation and description, corresponding to a fundamental ontology of descriptively various concrete particulars and events involving them. If anything in the recent literature of philosophy corresponds in point of *structure* to the skeleton of this primitive natural language ontology, it is the picture theory of the *Tractatus*, the relation of names and objects constituting, in their structural arrangement, the denotative link, and states of affairs representing the content when descriptively filled out.

From this sketch one derives a significant reminder: that the grammatical forms of discourse about abstract entities, fictional realms, moral and aesthetic domains – indeed all talk about anything – are the same as those deployed in talk of concrete particulars and their properties, and that an assertion about any subject matter takes the grammatical form of reference and predication. (In the analysis

---

[2]Thomas S. Maloney, *Roger Bacon on Signs*: Translated with an Introduction and Notes. *Mediaeval Sources in Translation* (Pontifical Institute of Mediaeval Studies 2013); M. Hauser, N. N. Chomsky and W. T. Fitch, 'The Faculty of Language: What Is It, Who Has It, and How Did It Evolve' *Science* 298 (2002); James R. Hurford, 'Nativist and Functional Explanations in Language Acquisition' in I. M. Roca (ed.) *Logical Issues in Language Acquisition* (Reidel 1995).

of utterances of other forces – imperatives, interrogatives, and so on – the phrastic is expressible in this form, the neustic involving supplementary indicators of mood, aspect and point.)

Familiarly, because the use of a referring expression carries, by virtue of its grammatical function, an apparent existential implication – the implication that *there is* the thing referred to – the 'surface form' of sentences used to make assertions is taken to be philosophically problematic, because all such uses about any subject-matter are misleadingly assimilated *via* the surface form to the base case of reference to concrete particulars in actual or possible perceptual environments. For convenience let us call this the Russellian view, for in the offing is the claim that an analysis is required that exposes the underlying logical form of the proposition or statement made by use of a natural language sentence in assertoric mode.[3]

To take the ontology-projecting nature of grammar to be misleading in this way is to assume that the 'real' ontology is chiefly if not only the one consisting of things in actual and possible perceptual environments, the other cases (abstract entities, fictional realms, etc.) at best by-courtesy ontologies to be implicitly understood as not 'real', at very least in the same sense. One can add that for nominalists about properties named in the base vocabulary, universals are likewise by-courtesy referents, mere conveniences for describing commonalities among instances of a given property.

However – and this is the important point – recall the observation in the previous chapter that fundamental physics and cognitive neuropsychology back the philosophical tradition which argues that the world of perceptual experience – the phenomenal world – is a virtual reality, such that we see that the ontology of the grammar of discourse about it is as much a projected ontology as is said to be

---

[3]The locus classicus is B. Russell, 'On Denoting' *Mind* 14(56) (1905): 469–493.

the case for abstract entities, fictional realms, and the rest; in short, an artefact of cognitive convenience for creatures of human scale and endowments. The Russellian view is that we mislead ourselves if we assimilate the ontological implications of the surface forms of grammar in non-perceptual discourses to the perceptual case; we see now that the perceptual case is on a par with those non-perceptual cases in projecting an ontology for its referring expressions. The assimilative relationship between the ontologies projected by grammar in domains of discourse other than the domain of concrete particulars therefore needs to be reversed, thus: the latter needs to be assimilated to the former instead. The point is general: all discourses project an ontology for their domains.

The fact that the ontology of discourse about perceptual environments has been privileged as what is 'real' while the other ontologies are ('merely') notional is not fully explained by appeal to practical considerations – for example, the inability to walk through walls or the undesirability of remaining in the path of oncoming buses – because there are direct analogies of these reality-insistent practicalities in the ontologies of other discourses. Anything with causally effective public presence in the world, for example institutions such as parliament and the law, are *ipso facto* as 'real' as a wall or a bus; anything indispensable to the intelligibility and functioning of a domain in which or by which a difference can be made, for example sets in mathematics, are as 'real' likewise, if these aspects of the characteristics of concrete particulars – independence of individual cognition of them, public accessibility, the resistance or robustness of their haecceity – enter into the definition of 'real', for these properties are possessed as much by sets and parliaments as by lumps of rock. These and other marks of the real are discussed more fully in due course (§8).

The fundamental claim here – that discourses project ontologies; that ontologies are discourse-relative – echoes such views as that existence is a theory-relative concept (in another guise, that the items in the ontology of a theory are whatever one is prepared to quantify over[4]). This is right, but it reminds us to distinguish between the question of what is to count as figuring *actually* in any domain as a subset of the totality of things that can be referred to in it, and those that do not. The ontology of a domain is the unsifted collection of all the referents in the discourse that ranges over it, but those referents which possess the property of satisfying specified conditions imposed by the canon of enquiry for the domain, are what count as *actual* for the domain: the existents in it.

And this point in turn generalises: not just the concept of existence but *therefore* the concepts of truth, reference and knowledge are discourse-relative, as following pages argue. One immediate source of philosophical difficulty vanishes upon acceptance of this, namely the difficulty that arises from thinking that the concept of the real is univocal across discourses, such that the question of where its limits of application lie among concrete, abstract and ideal referents is rendered especially pressing. Another philosophical difficulty is, however, thereby prompted for the domain of perceptual experience and whatever reducing domains are taken to have causal and explanatory relationships to it: namely, what is the basis of assignments to the category of the actual (of 'what exists') in that domain, and what does not ('horses *versus* unicorns' questions) – a question that reprises the debate about predications of 'exists' itself.

---

[4]In the offing, Rudolph Carnap, 'Empiricism, Semantics, and Ontology', *Revue Internationale de Philosophie* 4(11) (1950): 20–40, reprinted in Carnap, *Meaning and Necessity: A Study in Semantics and Modal Logic*, 2nd edn. (University of Chicago Press 1956) 205–221; W. V. Quine, 'On What There Is', *The Review of Metaphysics* 2(1) (1948): 21–38, reprinted in Quine, *From a Logical Point of View* (Harper 1953) 1–19.

As these remarks imply, the concepts of *actual* and *real* fall apart, as can be seen by noting the large difference between 'actual for a domain' (e.g. sets in mathematics) and 'ultimate reality' (the grail of metaphysical enquiry). To anticipate: a chair is actual, but not ultimately real; it is an actual (causal, encounterable, resistant, enduring) object in the virtual reality of perceptual experience.

A note on the concept of a 'discourse' as employed here is required. By 'discourse' is meant a region of thought and talk, an identifiably more or less coherent practice consisting in the embodiment and application of a scheme of concepts. A discourse always has an identity but rarely any sharp boundaries, because discourses overlap, interpenetrate and share conceptual resources. A list of individuable discourses, both incomplete and redundant, each item in it with its own subdiscourses and connections to others, would include: mathematical, scientific, moral, historical, fictional, perceptual, psychological/intentional, social, political and religious. The difficulty of constructing a neatly distinguished list is illustrated by the cluster 'social, moral, political, religious, psychological/intentional' given the multiple mutual interpenetrations of these and of these with 'historical, fictional' and even 'perceptual'; and as 'perceptual' connects with 'scientific' and 'scientific' with 'mathematical', any taxonomisation turns out as a blur of Venn diagrams. At the same time, each has its similarly blurred-boundary subdiscourses: 'religion' has not only different individual religions but these religions' internal divisions into sects and groupings; 'science' is an umbrella term for many specialist fields and specialist interdisciplinary fields; 'history' is highly subdivided by period and region, each with concepts specific to it – and so on.

Different principles might result in different taxonomies, but one which is of particular relevance here is a division between (a) those discourses in which the referring terms are taken to denote physical particulars and events in space and time or at least time, and (b) those that denote all other kinds of things (abstracta, intentional objects, fictional entities, etc.). Thus perception, history and science might cluster under the first heading, the rest under the second. This is rough, and immediately invites challenges: for example, if reference to psychological phenomena is shorthand for reference to complex neural events in the brain, why not include psychological discourse in (a)? This demands an account of reduction – and more precisely, remainderless reduction; where the contrasting idea of incomplete reductions of explanatory value might admit of property-emergence in the (partially)-reduced class. Another challenge might be to ask if any satisfactory definition of 'actual' must confine what is to fall under the (a) label, or whether that is too restrictive given the many attempts, attitudes and beliefs to the effect that there are non-(a) type things that are, by the light of the given attempts, actual.

The problem here is created by the long-standing objection to assimilating non-(a) discourses to (a) discourses on the grounds that surface grammar misleadingly prompts us to make existential commitments to the referents of subject terms in sentences. On the argument here, matters should be reversed: (a) discourses should be assimilated to non-(a) discourses as regards how reference is to be understood, with at the same time a separation of the question of what in the ontology ranged over by the discourse is to be accounted actual. This last is a matter for the canons of enquiry for the discourse to settle. On the former view, the mere act of referring is taken by itself to imply superficially that whatever one nominates in answering the question 'What are you talking about?' one is committed to treating as existent, and by this a host of philosophical perplexities is generated.

At this point it is informative – perhaps because some of the foregoing will prompt one to do so – to recall that the later Wittgenstein and Austen in their different ways argued that (to paraphrase) 'all is in order with ordinary language'.[5] The Wittgenstein of the *Investigations* sought to establish that ordinary language wears its logic on its sleeve; there is no underlying logical form which requires excavation to show what is 'really being said' – the Russellian view. Austen sought to dissolve the problem in an analogous way, by showing that such locutions as 'seems' and 'appears' used in accounts of perceptual experience convey an illegitimate *suggestio falsi*, and conflict with the facts about perceptual judgments (we do not say 'Looks like a pig, smells like a pig, therefore … ' we just say 'Lo! a pig'; Austen thus confusing the psychological and logical orders in perceptual judgment). Each had to qualify this view by requiring that proper attention must be paid to avoiding the assimilation of uses of expressions in one language game to their uses in others (Wittgenstein) and to nuances and subtleties of meaning (Austen). Presumably, in Wittgenstein's case, this was to avoid thinking that because the grammar of the sentences 'Horses have four legs' and 'Unicorns have one horn' is identical, unicorns exist. But this in turn is to privilege the ontology of discourse about things in perceptual environments. If one language game is ontologically privileged and other discourses have the potential to mislead in regard to what there is, then it is not correct to say that ordinary language is in order. Rather the contrary. But if ordinary language is in order because all discourses operate in the same way, then the question changes; it becomes the two related questions, 'Which if any ontology or ontologies is or are to be

---

[5]L. Wittgenstein, *Philosophical Investigations*, G. E. M. Anscombe and R. Rhees (eds.), G. E. M. Anscombe (trans.) (Blackwell 1953); J. L. Austen, *Sense and Sensibilia*, ed. G. J. Warnock (Oxford University Press 1962).

privileged, and how do we discriminate within them what is actual and what is not?'; and they have to be answered independently.

There is, however, a different and more important reason for questioning the claim that ordinary language is in order. This is that the basal conceptual scheme organising the ontology projected by talk of things in perceptual environments is not only projected for the convenience of creatures of human scale and endowments, but is for that very reason ad hoc and inconsistent: the case for this claim is offered shortly. Accordingly the surface forms of grammar, and not just these but the lexicons they deploy, are not, in any unqualified sense, 'in order'. In the case of the conceptual schemes that organise the ontologies of other discourses, matters differ: in some (for example, mathematics and logic) conscious attempts at consistency are made; in others (for example, the value discourses of ethics and aesthetics) the problem of the univocality of evaluative concepts arises (see §3). That this is so further implies that language, even extraordinary language (say, mathematics, quantum theory), is again not unqualifiedly 'in order'.

The observation that discourses project ontologies turns attention to the concepts of reference and truth at work in them, together with the epistemologies thus entailed.

In the case of talk about entities and events in environments of perceptual experience, a cluster of theories has been offered about how referring terms connect with their referents, and a cluster of theories has been offered about the nature of the relationship between mental contents in which reference is made to entities or events 'external' to them (that is, in a spatio-temporal realm whose existence and character are existentially independent of being intended by the act of perception or thought in question) which makes the content 'true' – the content expressible as an assertion or knowledge-claim about the referent – in every case in which the content, in one way or another, corresponds to it. The rider 'in one way or another' registers that different theories of truth in which truth is regarded as a substantive property of truth-bearers (whatever they are: propositions, statements, theories) consist in different ways of making out the correspondence relation, given the familiar difficulties attending efforts to flesh out the basic Aristotelian intuition that 'to say what is that it is, is true' by specifying the putatively corresponding relata.

'Reference' is here, as above, to be understood as a relation between a term (noun, name, description) and something other than itself (thing, event, state of affairs). The distinction between referring as something speakers do and denoting as the relation between a term and its referent is acknowledged, but as the discussion here entails, the intimacy of the connection between referring terms and uses of them not merely licences but necessitates a context-individuating movement between the senses.

The theories offered about the nature of reference and truth in discourse about items in perceptual environments are taken to be theories of reference and truth *tout court* – which is to say that 'reference' and 'truth' are taken to be univocal concepts, applicable in discourses other than the perceptual environment case also. To see why this is incorrect it is first useful to note some significant features of such theories in application to this case.

It is a natural starting assumption that being able to refer to some item (particular or event) x requires being able to identify x and thereby, or also, individuate it among other possible competitors to be the referent of the expression used on the occasion, in any circumstance beyond the immediate ostensively available presence and salience of the item being talked about. This entails that x satisfies identity conditions,[6] these consisting in identification and

---

[6] In the offing, Quine's 'no entity without identity' *Ontological Relativity and Other Essays* (Columbia University Press 1969) 23.

individuation conditions jointly, which in turn appears to entail that successful reference to x turns upon knowledge of how to identify and individuate x.

The phrase 'appears to entail' signals the first putative difficulty with this starting assumption, for the two reasons that it implies that reference is secured via knowledge of the applicability of at least some identifying descriptions – denied by such views as that referring terms are rigid designators, that whether or not reference is fixed by a baptismal use of descriptions it thereafter consists in a direct causal history of use to pick out uniquely the baptised entity – and that one can successfully refer to x by means of descriptions that do not apply (the referential as opposed to attributive case), or that one can even refer to x in complete ignorance of x, as when 'x' picks out some individual in a possible world in which x exists but lacks every property standardly associated with x, as in '"Aristotle" refers to Aristotle in the world in which he was not born in Stagira, did not study with Plato, did not tutor Alexander, wrote none of the works said to be authored by Aristotle, etc.'.

As a first step to supporting the claim that reference has to go *via* descriptive knowledge, one can note why the idea that reference to x can be made successfully even in complete ignorance of x seems so implausible even in the perceptual case. Suppose someone who knows neither astronomy nor Greek mythology, and therefore does not know that 'Callisto' names both a moon of Jupiter and a nymph in Greek mythology, ventures the remark, 'Callisto is interesting' (also implausibly, one has to leave aside questions about what might motivate such an utterance beyond arbitrary whim or accident, together with complicating possibilities such as that 'Callisto' happens also to be the name of a motor vehicle marque or a pop star, of which the speaker is also ignorant). To which is she referring on this view – the moon or the nymph? Or does she thereby refer to both? If it is the different question which of the moon or nympth the *name* as opposed to its use (on this or any occasion) denotes, the natural move is to say 'the name "Callisto" *can be used* to refer either to … ' But this is not to the point here, because the speaker has in fact uttered the name in order to predicate something of its referent, so it is this particular connection between the use of the name and a referent that is at issue. (To reinforce the point: If 'Callisto' also names a vehicle marque and a pop star, does she refer to all four?)

Vary the question: suppose she knows only that 'Callisto' refers to the mythological nymph, and is ignorant of astronomy; if she arbitrarily utters the words 'Callisto orbits Jupiter' has she thereby, given that she has 'said *something* true', referred to the second-largest moon of Jupiter despite only thinking that the name denotes the nymph?

The natural thought in all these cases is that she does not succeed in referring at all; that she refers to none of nymph, moon, marque or pop star for the key reason that she lacks requisite identifying knowledge of any of them.

Again: suppose the speaker does have some astronomical beliefs, but rather muddled ones, for she correctly associates the name 'Callisto' *qua* name of an astronomical body with the constellation Ursa Major, has also heard that one of the moons of Jupiter is named for the nymph, and therefore believes 'that Ursa Major is a satellite of Jupiter'. The 'referential-attributive' distinction allows a false belief to secure reference in the kind of case used to illustrate the difference (as in the woman 'drinking champagne' who is drinking sparkling water), but does it plausibly extend to this case, requiring us to ask whether *false* beliefs establish *correct* referential connections other than in ostensive circumstances? A reply might be: in the utterance 'Ursa Major orbits Jupiter' successful reference has been made to Ursa Major but something false has been said about it. But given that the *route* to Ursa

Major (the constellation as referent) in this act of referring involved a belief about its relation to Jupiter in significant part turning on the description 'satellite of Jupiter', in the absence of the kind of corrective supplement available in the Donnellan-type case ('the woman drinking champagne' – 'that's not champagne it's sparkling water' – 'oh well at any rate, her': ostension as fallback), it appears implausible to maintain that the speaker has successfully referred to Ursa Major. The (failed) parallel would be 'Ursa Major is a satellite of Jupiter' – 'No, it is not a satellite of Jupiter' – 'Oh well, at any rate, I mean Ursa Major'. If we enrich the case to allow that the speaker knows that Ursa Major is a constellation but bizarrely believes constellations can orbit planets, and utters a complex statement about it which mixes true and false elements, such as 'Ursa Major is a constellation sometimes known as the Big Dipper because of the asterism of its seven main stars, and it orbits Jupiter', the ground for saying that she successfully refers to Ursa Major but believes some false things about it, is that some of the descriptions she applies *because* she takes them to apply, in fact apply. In general, indeed, it is hard to see how to explain how a speaker can say something false about x without its being x which is successfully referred to, and in such a way that the falsehood does not derail referential access to x. This echoes the pretheoretical intuition that some minimum disjunction of descriptions must apply to a putative referent x if it is indeed x that is being referred to.

The idea that *sense* constitutes an epistemic route to a referent implies something more committal still, namely, that there is a minimum cluster of descriptions which are indispensable to identifying the referent.[7] The pretheoretical intuition in fact consists

---

[7] In the offing, Frege, Dummett: G. Frege, 'Über Sinn und Bedeutung.' In *Zeitschrift für Philosophie und philosophische Kritik*, 100 (1892): 25–50; translated as 'On Sense and Reference' by M. Black in Geach and Black (eds. and trans.), 1980, 56–78; M. Dummett, *The Interpretation of Frege's Philosophy* (Harvard University Press 1981).

in this view. By itself this does not entail commitment to essentialism (to real essences); it is contingently the case that Aristotle was born in Stagira, studied at Plato's Academy, wrote the *Nichomachean Ethics*, etc., but unless whatever is referred to by 'Aristotle' did at least some of these crucially identifying things it would not be *that* Aristotle who is referred to. Here perhaps one could invoke the distinction between nominal and real essences, respectively epistemological and metaphysical, and argue that some minimum cluster of descriptions constitutes the nominal essence required for security of reference.

Whatever the merits of these thoughts when discussed solely in the perceptual environment case, they become of pressing relevance upon recognising that in the case of all other discourses reference is *only* achievable *via* identifying and individuating descriptions; for if the discourse of perceptual environments is projective and ontology-constituting in the same way as all others are, then either: if the concept of reference is univocal across discourses, reference in the perceptual environment case is achieved *via* descriptions as in all other discourses, or the concept of reference in the perceptual environment case is specific to that case – is discourse-relative – in a way that makes the successful functioning of reference essentially contingent on a grasp of senses ultimately rooted in actual or possible perceptual acquaintance with referents.

But this disjunction is not exclusive. Reference in perceptual environment discourse might be description-mediated as in other discourses, but be discourse-relative in that the *kind* of recognitional capacities speakers need in order to apply descriptions – given that these are themselves perceptual or perception-related (e.g. by inference from perceptual activity; related to actual or possible perceptual acquaintance) – are specific to discourse about a realm of concrete spatio-temporal entities.

The same conclusion about discourse-relativity applies *a fortiori* to the concept of truth – which in turn figures reflexively in the account to be given of the discourse-relativity of reference. To see this, begin by noting how other predicates of evaluation function, for a chief example '__is good'.

Evidently '__is good' is shorthand for whatever justifies a positive evaluation of what is so described. A knife, a dog, a dinner, a state of health, an action performed by a person, is good if (respectively) it cuts well, is obedient, is tasty and nourishing, is free of disease or disability, is beneficial to anyone or anything affected by it. Thus '__is good' is a place-holder for these more finely descriptive properties, individuated by context. Recognising that 'good' is not univocal immediately removes temptations to hypostasise a referent for it – a universal, 'goodness', or an abstract entity (a Form or Idea), 'The Good'. Its employment expresses in every case the attitude that what is so described is positive in character, which is why a single place-holder can do duty for the context-dependent fuller account of what is being asserted in the different cases. This is to say what application of the predicate *implies*, not what 'good' *means*; what 'good' *means* is different in each discourse.

The same applies to '__is true'. The assertions "'2 + 2 = 4' is true', "'a cloud consists of condensed water vapour" is true', "'lying is frequently socially harmful" is true', are respectively mathematical, empirical and moral in subject matter; what it is for each quoted statement to be true is different in each case. Candidates that have been proposed for filling out '__is true' in each case are, again respectively (and just for example), '__is constructible', '__is verifiable', '__is desirable to believe'. This demonstrates that '__is true' is a placeholder, shorthand for more specific predicates, individuated by context, whose use in each case indicates that a relevant kind of reliance can be placed on what is asserted – for example, that the proposition (statement, theory) can be reliably predicated in further reasoning or taken as a basis for action.

On this view, truth is a substantive property of truth-bearers; more circumstantially, the properties which in different discourses can shorthandedly be predicated by using '__is true' are substantive properties of what they thus describe. This observation by itself entails that although the accounts variously given by minimalist theories of truth accurately speak to some of the services that the placeholder '__is true' perform – for example: marking agreement, abbreviating what would be long iterations of assertions, providing a predicate in sentential contexts requiring one, etc. – they do not show that this is all that '__is true' does; indeed, far from it. This observation also shows that truth is not a primitive or indefinable concept, each of the more explicit expressions for which talk of truth is shorthand requiring a full account of its own.[8] A fuller account of these points is given in §4.

Correlatively, what it is to refer to something in a domain differs by domain, because the way of knowing what has to be known in order to identify referents in different domains differs. In an allied vocabulary this would be put by saying that what it is to grasp the sense of an expression differs by discourse. Referring to the number four, a raindrop, and the moral quality of an action, are all cases of referring because they involve picking something out in order to say something about it, which is why the relational predicate '__refers to__' collects all such cases. But the recognitional capacities at work differ by domain. To use correctly the expression 'four' requires implicitly knowing such things as that the number four is composite,

---

[8]In the offing, Davidson's theory of truth as primitive and indefinable: D. Davidson, 'The Folly of Trying to Define Truth' *Journal of Philosophy* Vol. XCIII (1996) and *Truth and Predication* (Belknap Press 2005). See Grayling, 'Truth and Indefinability' in *Truth, Meaning and Realism* (Continuum 2007) 39–54 and *passim*.

even, the successor of three and predecessor of five; to feel a drop of water on one's head and to identify it as a raindrop rather than a drop of water splashed from a nearby fountain is to know about rain, the behaviour of water in dynamic conditions, and some general facts about water itself; to talk about the moral quality of an action is to have a repertoire of beliefs and attitudes about the kinds of human behaviour that (to put the point at its most general) affect the welfare of sentient beings (and arguably the environment in general). A corpus of knowledge, different in each case, and different in *kind*, is presupposed to successful reference in each case.

Considerations of truth and reference come together in the fact that the corpora of knowledge required for successful reference to items in a given domain are in play in judgments of the truth-value of assertions about them. Ascertaining the truth-value of an assertion about how things are with some referent in a domain requires knowing enough to refer to it; the truth-values of assertions about a referent in a domain are referent-dependent. This would be the case in a causal theory of reference also, barely considered, in that in this theory successful reference turns on the history of association of the term with the referent and not on speaker's knowledge of identifying descriptions; the difference is that the causal view restricts 'refers' to what expressions do independently of speakers, even (theoretically but very unintuitively) *tout court* as when a term has been, say, forgotten through desuetude – e.g. 'phlegmasia', a currently unused medical term meaning 'inflammation' but now, sequestered in old medical dictionaries, inert and unknown; yet even if no-one uses or knows how to use it, says the causal theorist, it nevertheless refers to inflammation – whereas the descriptive view requires that the relation between a referring term and its referent requires of the term's user that she knows that the term thus refers *because* she can identify its referent. If she uses a referring term without knowing what it refers to – literally: she does not know what she is talking about – *she* cannot be said to be referring to what the *term* denotes, and accordingly her assertion cannot be granted a truth-value, *pace* the observation that she might have 'said something true' for if so it will have been by accident. For the fact that the *term* so denotes is not a matter independent of speakers in general: indeed, how could it possibly be so? That 'phlegmasia' refers to inflammation is the result of having been coined for this purpose by medical practitioners of yore; its reference is a function of *their* identifying knowledge. In the quarrel between causal and descriptivist theories the fact that the latter incorporates the former but *via* a knowledge condition is obscured – here taking what is correct from the causal theory, viz. that 'phlegmasia' denotes a diseased state of animal tissue even if, currently unused by any speaker, it sits inert on the page of a dictionary. But this is because the referential link between 'phlegmasia' and inflammation is the precipitate of a practice of speakers' uses of the word to refer to phlegmasia *via* their identifying knowledge of it; the word-world link is established by the convention that thus arises, and reference to the practice – crucially including the application of knowledge in which it consists – is ineliminable.[9]

These thoughts, together with the expansion of the points about truth in relation to assertion in §4, provide a first step towards making out the argument here. The next is to link them to considerations about the conceptual schemes embodied in discourses.

---

[9]Grayling, 'Explicit Speaker Theory' in *Truth, Meaning and Realism* (Continuum 2007).

§ 3

Conceptual Schemes

The purpose of this chapter is to demonstrate that the conceptual scheme of perceptual experience is an ad hoc, pragmatic and paraconsistent set of structures devised to organise experience as enjoyed by creatures at the scale and with the cognitive endowments of human beings. I employ the term 'paraconsistent', here borrowed and adapted from the formal case of logics that can tolerate contradiction non-explosively (i.e. without licensing any conclusion *ad libitum*), to bear an extended informal sense of 'involving conceptual commitments non-trivially but generally non-explosively either inconsistent or incommensurable'.[1] Apart from the intrinsic interest of the point, it is a highly consequential one. The traditional and still prevailing view that the conceptual scheme of perceptual experience is – more or less, or at least adjustably – coherent and consistent, that it reflects, reveals or entails information about reality as it exists independently of the cognitive activities of perceivers, and that it is consistent with (can non-metaphorically and without serious

---

[1]There are however cases where explosions occur; in the functioning of the scheme they are typically ignored, 'lived with'; in philosophy they generate attempts at reductions, even those which are incomplete. See §6. The scheme is not dialethic in the sense that statements made within its context are true and false simultaneously; paraconsistent statements are both true when true, the constraint is that the disjunctive syllogism is inappropriate to their pairing. This does not block but in signal cases can prompt reductive efforts.

remainder take translations from and be reduced to) fundamental science, is the source of a number of persistent philosophical problems about truth, reference and knowledge – and, to boot, the explanation of why interpretations of quantum theory are at best only heuristically possible in classical terms.

Results in cognitive neuropsychology, which investigates the cognitive structures (most plausibly to be regarded as devised by evolutionary pressures) that organise input of sensory data, provides parallel support for the claim that the scheme is ad hoc and pragmatic. An evolutionary story would make this fact unsurprising. The role of cognitive modalities in creating mental models of the perceptual environment by supplementing sensory input – the filling-in of the blind spot in the visual field is a simple and familiar example – is well understood. Neurophilosophy's invocation of empirical results accordingly predicates their observations to this effect.[2] Consideration of developments in both fundamental science on the microstructure and properties of the physical universe, and in cognitive neuropsychology on mental modelling of the perceptual environment, illustrate how the world of perceptual experience is a 'virtual reality' in almost exactly the sense in which the realm created by a virtual reality headset is so.

The insights in play are not new; they have long been recognised in the philosophical tradition. Aristotle's postulation of the 'common sense' which integrates data from the five traditional sensory modalities, and much more circumstantially Kant's epistemology in which concepts of the understanding organise spatio-temporally conditioned intuitions into phenomenal reality, are anticipators of neuropsychology in this respect. In recognising phenomenal reality

---

[2]An example: S. S. Gouveia and G. Northoff, 'A Neurophilosophical Approach to Perception' in D. Shottenkirk, M. Curado, and S. S. Gouveia (eds.) *Perception, Cognition and Aesthetics* (Routledge/Taylor & Francis Group 2019) 41–63.

as a virtual reality, cognitive neuropsychology aligns with views from Parmenides and Plato through Berkeley and Kant to recent phenomenalism, all of which are attempts to provide a metaphysics for the epistemology thus premised.[3]

It will rightly be pointed out that the terms of the (putatively 'the') human conceptual scheme undoubtedly take different glosses in different cultures, but as the point about neuropsychology shows, the fundamental cognitive architecture of the human brain and mind – 'brain-mind' is sometimes used as a clumsy shorthand for recognising the conflicting commitments that, first, mental phenomena are products of brain activity and, second, that brains are themselves phenomena, thus constituents of the virtual reality we bootstrappingly take it that brains themselves create – underlies all such glosses, and we are entitled to speak of a basal conceptual scheme which expresses itself in terms of a natural language ontology of things and their properties, however glossed (thus allowing that *that thing there* identifiable by its brilliance and apparent movement across the sky – the sun – might be analogised as a deity-driven chariot in Greek mythology and theorised as a giant ball of burning hydrogen and helium by modern science, but is still 'that thing there' eye-searingly brilliant and repeatedly and regularly seeming to move from the roughly eastern to the roughly western horizon).

The following demonstration of the ad hoc nature of the conceptual scheme of perceptual experience – henceforth just 'scheme'; schemes that organise other domains of discourse will be qualified as such – focuses upon three claims. One is that incommensurable subdiscourses are applied to the same phenomena, their use dependent upon an interest or need different from the interest or need prompting use of

---

[3]A. C. Grayling, *Berkeley: The Central Arguments* (Duckworth 1976); 'Russell, Experience and the Roots of Science' in N. Griffin, *The Cambridge Companion to Bertrand Russell* (Cambridge: Cambridge University Press 2003).

the other discourse. The second is that important structural elements of the scheme such as the concept of time consist in multiple and non-overlapping sub-concepts and are essentially dependent on metaphor for their utility. The third is that generic expressions (including words like 'thing' and placeholder predicates like '__is true', '__is nice'), general terms and vagueness show that how phenomena are collected and organised meet needs specific to creatures of human scale and endowments independently of how anything external to experience is configured.

Before taking each of the three claims in turn, some clarification of the terms 'scale', 'human endowments', and 'organisation of experience by concepts' is pertinent.

If we take the Planck length (1.6×10^{-35}m) and the diameter of the observable universe (93.016 billion light years, 2×10^{26}m) as the currently known lower and upper limits of size by length in the universe, then human beings at a world average height of 1.65m are closer to the cosmological than the Planck scale. This accords with the fact that unaided human cognitive capacity can register the existence and properties of objects many times larger than human beings, but not objects smaller by much less of a factor: the moon is 263,000 times larger than a human being, a single molecule of water 1000 times smaller than a human being, and yet the first is clearly visible to the naked eye while the latter is invisible without instrumental help. Notice that this claim concerns *cognitive capacity* not *sensory equipment*, for of course a single photon (as photons are massless wave-particle dualities their 'size' is tricky to define but can be estimated as 1.0006×10^{30} times smaller than an atom) can be registered by the human retina, though it takes between 5 and 10 photons to strike the retina in a period of less than ten milliseconds for them to be consciously registered. According to inflationary theory the actual universe is very much larger than the observable universe, which shifts downwards the point at which the human scale is located in the relative size of things. But whatever that point is, it is at an extremely thin slice of the overall scale of the universe.

A familiar thought-game enables us to recognise that even at this narrow scale we account for different ways of organising the phenomena met with: a house, a room in the house, the furniture in the room, the individual chairs and tables, the molecules of wood and other materials of which the chairs and tables are made, the atoms constituting the molecules, the hadrons (protons and neutrons) of the nucleus and the envelope of electrons constituting atoms, the gauge bosons mediating the forces, the quarks constituting hadrons, and so on downwards in scale perhaps to strings. What is referred to depends upon the interest and purpose of referring to them in the given way; the question, 'Which level is *the* "real" level at which these phenomena exist' makes sense only against a background assumption to the effect that (say) quarks and leptons, or strings, or fluctuations in the quantum field, are the final reduced level of physical reality. Familiarly, what is postulated as the ontology of current best theory is a tendentious place to locate 'ultimate reality', because the temptation to move an instrumentalist view of the ontology successively downwards to smaller scales is ever present. (No Machian would now regard protons as merely instrumentally-conceived theoretical entities, given that they are smashed together at CERN on an actual as well as regular basis at high energies; but the status of strings is not – yet, perhaps – equivalently secure.) Yet the house, the room, the furniture, are all 'real' *in sensu* 'actual' (though not 'ultimately real') in a perfectly acceptable use of this term, and their reality meets the interests of creatures of human scale better than adequately.

An allied point can be made by considering cultural ways of carving up the world of experience for human convenience. Suppose a Star Trek beam machine instantaneously transports a native of the Amazon jungle into the book stacks of the Library of Congress. Supposing him never to have been in a library or encountered books before, one has to ask why, confronted by a shelf of books, he would regard it as an array of individual items rather than a single multi-coloured object like a large snake or caiman. Even if a modicum of subsequent experience demonstrated that the books are individual items arranged in a row, the assumption that they had, before being cut up into smaller slices, been components of a single bookshelf-long entity, would not be corrected until further complex experiences had been undergone. Absent these latter, if the beam machine in just a few moments reversed its activity and deposited the man back in the jungle, his view about what he had encountered would remain as it was first formed. The example speaks to the question of how and why the world is carved up in the way it standardly is in the basal ontology of the conceptual scheme – namely, by annexing the answer to practical interests, which differ by need and context.

A consideration to take away from these remarks is that the point of origin of the human perspective on the universe is such that it is like trying to see the world of everyday experience through a pinhole, unless aided by instruments pushed, as it were, through the pinhole to gather information otherwise inaccessible on its distal side. In the case of scientific investigation of the structure and properties of physical phenomena at the microscopic and cosmic scales, the instruments deployed are themselves limited in capacity by their manufacture at the human scale, and the information they provide is interpretable – if at all – by concepts formed and applicable at the human scale, both of these on the proximal side of the pinhole. This 'pinhole' analogy – a better alternative name is the 'classical horizon', on the human-scale proximal side constituting the world of perceptual experience while on the ultramicroscopic and cosmic scales of the distal side constituting the domains of the relevant scientific discourses –

becomes of particular significance in §7 in discussing the lessons epistemological scepticism teaches about the nature of enquiry, and in raising the interesting question of what we learn about the classical horizon from those sciences which, so to speak, straddle it (for a chief example, biochemistry).

Meanwhile, we see that even at the human scale the ontology of perceptual experience is an artefact of interests at that scale, different ontologies at different subscales applied according to what interest is in play. The view that our concepts of natural kinds, in particular, show that nature is carved at *its* joints and not at our convenience, is contested by this claim; this is discussed in §6.

The three claims mentioned above in support of the view that the conceptual scheme is an ad hoc patchwork affair – the role of incommensurable subdiscourses addressed to the same phenomena, the multiple and non-overlapping nature of structural elements of the scheme, and the use of vague terms and general terms – are taken in turn, as follows.

A single example suffices to establish the point that discourses applied to the 'same' phenomena can be incommensurable, that is, neither mutually intertranslatable nor reducible one to the other. Consider a physicist and a sociologist observing a series of events unfolding on a field before them. The physicist describes the events in terms of bodies with certain masses moving at certain velocities, interacting according to the principles of mechanics and emitting radiation at certain frequencies. The sociologist describes the events as a football game. She might speak of a field goal, a team coach, a penalty, the purposes of a scrimmage, the significance of a 'fourth down'. The meaning of what she says turns on the intentional concepts she employs, none of which are translatable into concepts of mass, velocity and radiation. Is there a remainderless reduction of the thought, 'The coach did not want offence to use that play at that point' to the level of the atomic constitution of neurons in the brain? To regard the two discourses as ultimately commensurable requires accepting the possibility of such a reduction. But the content of that thought is not and cannot be narrow, such that a neuropsychologist could look at the microstructure of the brain and identify that particular thought in the electro-chemical activity observable there; to individuate the thought as that particular thought requires knowing something about football in the world beyond the brain – which is to say that the content of the thought is broad (invoking here the broad content-narrow content distinction as for example applied in Twin Earth debates). The irreducibility of intentional concepts to physical ones in this way is what the incommensurability of the two discourses consists in.

Claims like this immediately ring alarm bells in implying, at the very least, property-dualism about mental and physical phenomena – if not worse. By the end of the discussion here it will be seen that mind-body problems are a prime example of confected philosophical difficulties, because once one accepts that the ontologies of body-talk and mind-talk are equally projected by the discourses that find them convenient for organising the arenas of experience particular to each, the problem dissolves; it was created in the first place by attempting to assimilate the ontologies of the two discourses and univocally applying the concepts of reference and existence to the resulting hybrid. The point generalises well beyond the mind-body case: wherever problems arise about the commensurability of discourses or the reducibility of ontologies (a physicist's description of the buildings and their occupants, together with their occupants' movements and radiations within the building, which a sociologist describes as 'Parliament in session', is another example of very many that could be adduced), the resolution of the apparent dilemma is to recognise that interest determines discourse, and discourse projects ontology, each ontology ultimate (ultimate enough, one might say) for the interest. The problem lies not in assuming that there is one privileged ontology that is ultimate in relation to them all, but in the wrong choice of which ontology to serve as ultimate in the current state of theory and action.

The foregoing considerations by themselves demonstrate the patchwork nature of the scheme, which can be likened to a toolbox; for nails, a hammer; for screws, a screwdriver; trying to 'reduce' a hammer to a screwdriver or vice versa misses the point. Another demonstration is provided by the diversity of uses among expressions used to address different features of the same thing, a prime example being the vocabulary of time and the different things we think about time and temporal experience, and what we use the discourses of time to do.

First, an assemblage of reminders about time. It is a commonplace of temporal experience that subjective perceptions of the passage of time differ. The same event that pleases one person but bores her companion (an evening at the opera, perhaps) can go like a flash to the former but take excruciatingly long to the latter.[4] To coordinate subjectively different lengths of time to each other, public time is established by reference to regular saliences observable to all – the daily passage of the sun, the monthly phases of the moon. Because measurements based on the sun and moon are approximate and they fluctuate – the length of days vary with the seasons, lunar months do

---

[4]In this connection one can adduce considerations about distortions in perception of the passage of time, such as the Alice in Wonderland Syndrome; see A. Weissenstein et al., 'Alice in Wonderland Syndrome' *Journal of Pediatric Neurosciences* 9(3) (2014).

not fit exactly to the solar year – a more accurate system is necessary.[5] Public time is now measured precisely by atomic clocks, one second in SI units defined as the period in which a Caesium-133 atom oscillates.[6]

The prescriptive nature of public time is well exemplified by the history of railway timetables. In Britain the Mean Times of Bristol and Cardiff were respectively 10 minutes and 13 minutes behind Greenwich Mean Time (GMT), so in 1847 the Railway Clearing House adopted GMT as standard for the network; by the mid-1850s almost all public clocks in the kingdom were set to GMT and in 1880 Parliament established GMT as the official national standard. It accordingly became the international benchmark because of the geographical extent of British imperial possessions. This is stipulative public time. But the advance from subjective to public time, however precisely the latter is defined, does not yield 'objective' or 'absolute' time of the kind assumed by Newton (time as an 'empty container' existing independently of events within it). Locke postulated that absolute time is conceived by extrapolating indefinitely forward and backwards from public time, but as the adverb itself implies, this does not yield absolute time (nor, which is different again, infinite time) but only indefinite time – a temporal series without identifiable limits fore or aft.[7] Clarke, in the correspondence with Leibniz, defended the Newtonian conception against Leibniz's relational view (time as

---

[5]The solar year is 365.24219 days, the lunar month 29 days, hence the reason for calendar months being 30 or 31 days except for February at 28 days, extended to 29 every leap year to adjust for the drift of the calendar from the solar year.

[6]In the period its activity (at its ground state) defines, Caesium-133 oscillates slightly over nine billion times, giving an accuracy to within 1/15 billionth of a second per year. At an MIT lab it has been proposed that vastly more precise measurements can be obtained by entangling several hundred ytterbium atoms, which vibrate 100,000 times faster than caesium.

[7]See John Locke, *An Essay Concerning Human Understanding* II.xv.5 (1689).

a linear and anisotropic 'order of successions').[8] In all these cases the assumption at work is that 'time' is a univocal concept susceptible to definition as such.

But the widening difference in subsequent debates between philosophical attention to temporal phenomena – time as experienced – and physical theory is marked. Such notions as Bergsonian 'duration' and the idea of the 'specious present' address the subjective experience of time, while the absorption of time into Minkowski space in which time is the fourth dimension of a continuum (taking 'dimension' to refer to the smallest number of coordinates required to locate a point in a mathematical space) serves the purposes of the general theory of relativity's account of gravity. Suggested by the conception of spacetime as a continuum, such notions as 'spacetime worms' (the path of an individual entity through the continuum), perdurantism and 'temporal parts', and conceptions of universal time such as the Block and Growing Block theories, have been predictable developments. On the Block Universe view, all times (past, present and future) exist together; on the Growing Block view, past and present are real but the future does not yet exist – or more accurately: that the future is open, and its becoming present and past consists in the progressive accumulation of existents.[9]

These competing views turn on the choice of a specified conception of time, once again as if 'the concept of time' is univocal in each and such that the preferred definition – time as eternal, or as a moving one-directional arrow, as explicable via the concept of entropy, as a

---

[8]See Samuel Clarke, *The Leibniz-Clarke Correspondence*, ed. H. G. Alexander (Manchester University Press 1956). Though a significant part of this debate relied on theological considerations, the use made by Leibniz of his Principle of Sufficient Reason – which Clarke accepted – and the Identity of Indiscernables retains a live interest.

[9]For a way into the predictable complexification of debate about the Growing Block view, see Roberto Loss, 'Open Future, Supervaluationism and the Growing-Block Theory: A Stage-Theoretical Account' *Synthese* 199 (2021).

set of relations, as a dimension of a continuum – makes independent sense. The purpose here is not to assess the merits of competing theories of this kind, philosophical or physical, but to note that no univocal conception is available in the conceptual scheme to serve as its privileged source. This is because how temporal concepts function in the scheme exhibits a variety in ways of being interpreted and applied. As structural features of the scheme, the differences in the uses made of temporal concepts – subjective, public, objective, physical – are ineliminable and mutually irreducible by anything other than an *incomplete* reduction (see §6). This is shown by the complexity of relations between subdiscourses of time, something well illustrated by the McTaggart argument.[10]

McTaggart took his argument to establish the unreality of time. Instead it shows that different ways of talking about the place and order of events in time address different interests we have in employing such talk. A-series concepts (past, present, future) presuppose the idea of change and accord naturally with dynamic conceptions such as the Growing Block theory; utterances attributing temporal location are tensed, and their truth-values change according to when they are indexed. B-series concepts (earlier, later) are applied in tenseless utterances, retain their truth-values eternally, and accord naturally with a Block Universe conception. McTaggart took the A-series to be fundamental – the B-series being insufficient because static, omitting the essential element of change – and yet inconsistent because all three properties of being past, being present and being future apply to all events, yet no two can belong to any event together.

The alleged inconsistency of the A-series vanishes when it is recognised what work the B-series does in the truth-condition for

---

[10]J. M. E. McTaggart, 'The Unreality of Time', *Mind* 17 (1908): 457–73; reprinted in McTaggart, *The Nature of Existence*, Vol. 2 (Cambridge University Press 1927).

utterances in which one of the A-series properties is predicated. Possession of a truth-value by an A-property-predicating statement requires fulfilment of a presupposition, viz. security of a reference point in time in relation to which the predication applies in B-series terms, viz. earlier or later, thus: the statement 'event e happened in the past' can itself only be true or false if it is true that at the time of its utterance e is later than the event in question. And likewise, *mutatis mutandis*, for the other properties. In this way the A-series is parasitic on the B-series, a point in any case obvious: the only way to explain the relations between the A-properties themselves is by saying how they stand in B-series terms with respect to each other.

The point generalises to tenses themselves. Take the categories of the Latin conjugations as a simple model: present (I run), future (I will run), imperfect (I was running), perfect (I ran), future perfect (I will have run), pluperfect (I had run). For the future perfect and the pluperfect, B-series concepts are essential: 'I will have run' applies to a point in time x after an earlier point in time y which latter is itself later than the time of utterance, while 'I had run' applies to a point in time x before a later point in time y itself earlier than the time of utterance. Obviously, talk of the future relates to a time or times later than the time of utterance. Less obviously but arguably, the B-series is involved in aspect also (as involved in the imperfect and perfect tenses, respectively denoting durations incomplete and completed) in at least the sense that in both not only is reference made to a time earlier than the time of utterance, but in what manner the event bears that relation to the time of utterance.

Asymmetry in the application of B-series concepts to the A-series enters with the present: the present is neither earlier nor later than any given time other than itself but a defining combination of these, reciprocally requiring the A-series: any 'now' is earlier than any future relative to it, later than any past relative to it. Given that attempts to define 'now' typically concede to the intuition that any moment has duration such that anything intelligibly describable as 'now' comprehends some moving fraction of past and future within it (the more so because all uses of 'now' are context-dependent; they can refer not just to a present moment but, say, to the present year or decade), the claim that B-dependent A-series concepts are at work here too is irresistible.

Another and fuller way to analyse the relativity of tenses is to employ the contrast drawn by Reichenbach and elaborated by Comrie between 'speech time', 'event time' and 'reference time',[11] while the further complexities of expressions turning on uses of 'next', 'since', 'until', 'began', 'finished', 'simultaneous', 'during', reference to instants and periods, and problems about the truth-value of future-tensed statements (Aristotle's sea-battle), receive detailed examination both in discussions of temporal logic and in metaphysics.[12] The wealth of insights in these debates is great; here the focus is exclusively on the fact that the dominating factor in the conceptual scheme's array of temporal concepts is utility, such that on some occasions reference is made to an instant and on others to a period, on some occasions precisely and on others vaguely (think of uses of 'simultaneous', 'after') – in general, communicative intention and context enter essentially into the interpretation of a temporal term's application on an occasion, such that (for example) 'then' in 'it happened then' could refer to an instant or a century, 'at the same time' to an exact coincidence in time or in the course of a century – and so on.

---

[11] H. Reichenbach, *Elements of Symbolic Logic* (Dover Publications, Inc. 1947) Ch. 6 and *passim*; B. Comrie, *Tense* (Cambridge University Press 1985).

[12] A window into the extensive literature is provided by the two volumes of P. Blackburn, P. Hasle and P. Øhrstrøm (eds.), *Logic and Philosophy of Time* (Aalborg University Press 2019); C. Callender, *The Oxford Handbook of the Philosophy of Time* (Oxford University Press 2013).

If these points are implied by the simpler case of the connection between A-series and B-series concepts as discussed above, they apply *a fortiori* to the more elaborate cases considered in the metaphysical and logical debates mentioned. But accepting – if one does – that one cannot explain the terms of the A-series without reference to the B-series turns out to be not yet the whole story, for the difference in their respective manner of possessing truth-value is significant. The observation that statements predicating A-series properties change in truth value with changes in temporal standpoint whereas B-series predications have their truth-values eternally, registers an important feature of their respective places in cognitive economy. In marking a difference between an A-series task of ascribing an order to events relatively, the order in question being temporary, and the knowledge in B-series terms that events are ordered as earlier or later absolutely, entails a difference in the logical properties of knowledge claims involving temporal reference. The two cases differ crucially in that to *know p* in the A-series case requires knowing something else q specifically about the temporal location relevant to the subject-matter, whereas knowing p in the B-series case presupposes no such thing. Occupancy of different positions in inferential frameworks is a significant matter, given that in varying according to how temporal relations are referenced the truth-conditions of tensed and untensed assertions require respectively independent mastery. A typical set of assumptions is that statements about the past have definite truth-value, those about the future have none, while those about the local and immediate present pose a challenge as to choice of treatment: either they are always in effect statements about an immediate past, viz. the verifying or confirming just-current ground for assignment of truth-value (even when 'the present' is an extended period – this year, this decade – with the 'immediate' past being extended accordingly), or they are vague, and the question of their truth-value, or whether

     The Metaphysics of Experience

they have one at all, falls into the in-tray of problems about vagueness (on which, more shortly).

If grasp of the meaning of sentences in the language consists in or at least essentially involves grasp of truth or assertibility conditions, then mastery of future-tensed discourse can be represented in possible-worlds terms as a disjunction of determinately true versions and determinately false versions distributed across selected worlds. This avoids accepting truth-value gaps for future-tensed statements, but introduces a further ineliminable asymmetry between them and past-tensed statements, which apply to a single world – the actual one – and have a determinate truth-value, and present-tensed statements, with the problematic choice about them just described. In connection with the ad hoc nature of the scheme, the implication to be noted is that to learn to talk of time is accordingly to learn more than one subdiscourse of time in which different rules apply.

Moreover, the different ways of talking about time are not coterminous in their applications beyond talk of time-relations. For a chief example, the B-series plays a more fundamental role in causal thinking than the A-series. The causal relation is dynamic, takes place in or over time, but the temporal relations between causes and effects are strictly B-series (including 'simultaneous' in the series, convenient for cases where cause and effect are held to occur together).[13] What this shows is that the difference between the concepts in the two series does not demonstrate the 'unreality of time' as if 'time' denoted a postulated single something shown by these considerations to be non-existent, but rather the relation (to employ the toolkit metaphor again) of different tools: in this case, rather aptly, a spanner and a screwdriver – for they can be used together, a spanner holding a bolt firm as a

---

[13]M. Huemer and B. Kovitz, 'Causation as Simultaneous and Continuous' *Philosophical Quarterly* 53 (2003): 556–65.

screwdriver is used to insert a screw into it (e.g. the dependence of the A-series concepts on the B-series concepts: 'present is later than past, earlier than future'), but each of them having independent uses besides (e g. A-series and change, B-series and causation, the former usable in an account of causal dynamics, the latter in discriminating causes from effects, capturing the facts that causal events *involve* change, but statements about causal nexuses are *about* a change).

Another important consideration is the intimate connection between conceptions of space and time in which the latter depends in *essentially* metaphorical ways on the former. It is a commonplace that distances are expressible in temporal terms – 'the airport is thirty minutes away' – when citing the geographical distance alone has nugatory informative content, given that fifteen miles on a desert road and fifteen miles from a city centre to an airport are very different matters. The description of the distance as effective distance in the city context requires reference to time to be useful, while reference to time is inessential in the desert road case. Whereas here space is being described in temporal terms, the reverse occurs with complete generality in speaking of time intervals as lengths – 'long' and 'short' – and in inferring the significance of more explicit measures of time: one minute is a short period of time relative to a century, a long period of time in the dental chair.

The primary signification of 'length' is a spatial extent between points in space; in dictionary definitions – reports of usage – the application to time is pertinently given as secondary or derived. Moreover judgments of the length of periods of time turn on the idea of spatial occupancy; a period of time containing little individual incident is described on a line in a shorter message than one that describes on a line a period crammed with incident – for example: contrast accounts of the period from the beginning of settled agriculture in the Neolithic era, about 10,000 BCE, to the 'rise of civilization' in Sumer after 4000 BCE, with accounts of the period from the latter date to the Bronze Age Collapse in 1200 BCE. The message on a line representing the former period is very considerably shorter than that representing the latter period, for the reason that greatly more is known about the latter period. (Use of the term 'message' here borrows from discussions of the contrast between simplicity and complexity, in which the length of message is one way of distinguishing between the two.[14]) Visualise a timeline along which the segment lengths are proportional to the quantity of information available for each point; like one of those representations of the human body proportioned to the degree of sensitivity to the physical environment showing enormous hands and lips, the timeline would for some periods represent many centuries as a short segment and individual decades as very long, thus representing the way time is viewed – how history is experienced, one could say, consistently with both a Block and a Growing Block perspective on it – as a space occupied by events.

For the purposes here the significant point is the irreducibility of the spatial metaphor in deployment of temporal concepts; all times are durations of some proportion (leaving aside the idealisation of a 'point-instant') and descriptions of durations essentially employ the spatial metaphor which applicable variants of 'length' such as 'extent', 'expanse', 'sweep' and 'stretch' – consider also 'long ago', 'far off', 'close', 'near', and the spatial connotation of 'immediate' – not only do not disguise but reinforce. We use the space-based concept of motion to speak also of events in time 'approaching', 'moving', 'standing still'.

---

[14]A competing way is length of evolutionary history; something might be simple by one measure and complex by the other, as one sees on considering a pebble on a beach which has a simple smooth round shape because of a long formation by wave action – a short message describes the shape, a long message describes the process by which the pebble acquired the shape.

This point generalises: the irreducible use of metaphor in the identifying knowledge required for reference and the descriptive resources applied in predications is as present in talk of the environment of perceptual experience generally as it is in other discourses, in these latter even more obviously reliant, in turn, on metaphorical uses drawn from the perceptual case itself. On this significant point, more later (§5).

Of the wide palette of terms and devices available in natural language for achieving its users' communicative ends, general terms and vague terms (not coterminous sets), and by courtesy of them general concepts and vague concepts, invite particular attention for the present purpose of illustrating the scheme's ad hoc nature. Both kinds of concepts are of great significance in the organisation of experience, as correlatively therefore are the terms that introduce them for facility of communication.

A useful preliminary is afforded by colour terms.[15] Consider 'red'. There is no such thing as *red* just as such in the world, only particular hues, tonalities and saturations of red: rose, vermilion, scarlet, maroon, crimson, carmine, blood, cinnabar, russet are a few; the interior design industry identifies over a thousand individuable colours across the part of the electromagnetic spectrum accessible to normal human vision. On the borders where red merges into orange it is not immediately obvious what to call the colour or colours that thus appear; for brevity speakers might typically use such locutions as 'reddy-orange' or 'orangey-red', or one of the designer's prescriptive coinings modified by intensifier or detensifier expressions. One could imagine a terminology being invented for ordinary uses after the fashion of compass points: 'north, north by east, north-north-east,

---

[15]This discussion draws on Bernard Harrison's discussion of Schlick in *Form and Content* (Blackwell 1973). The particular point at issue here was discussed at an Ockham Society meeting in Oxford in the late 1970s between Harrison, Gareth Evans and the author.

north-east by north' and so for all the rest of the thirty-two points thus designated – by analogy therefore 'red, red by orange, red-red-orange, red-orange by red' – but the interior design industry goes further in allocating codes to particular tints and intensities, just as navigators use degrees on the compass dial for the increased precision required for bearings, such as 'N 3° E'. However, the precisifications thus attained are, although non-arbitrary, *stipulative*: a hard border is introduced by fiat of necessity. Special subdiscourses (the colour language of the interior decoration industry, directions and orientations in navigation) dispense with the imprecisions of ordinary discourse because of the special needs they serve. But it is – so to say – the special need of everyday communication to be vague and general in order to be brief and effective, hence comparable precisification of vague and general terms typically defeats the object.

An example in support of this point: suppose someone comes into your bedroom at 2 am and wakes you by saying 'Fire'. It would not do to continue abed in sleepy contemplation of the wide range of application of the term, from the flame at the end of a match to the cheerful Yule log to the Great Fire of London to the thermonuclear reactions in the sun. Context, the circumstances of utterance of the term, the manner in which it is used, convey that some part of the house is ablaze and that this is information to be acted upon promptly. If the informant had taken time to specify in detail the location, the cause, the extent of the fire when he last saw it, the probable temperature so far reached, the proximity of other combustible materials, whether or not the fire brigade had been alerted, who had answered the call, what they had asked, and the estimated time of the brigade's arrival – if all this precisification had been indulged to ensure that the message 'Fire!' was as precise as 'N 3° E' or the HTML colour code '#C62828 198 40 40' for a standard shade of red, the object of the utterance would be fatally defeated.

From this we see that precisification of general and vague concepts and their introducing terminologies – allowing that for successful identification of a topic of discourse (for successful reference) what is said and context together must be informationally sufficient to serve that end – subverts the normal ends of their use, and at the same time that if precisification of them proves necessary in special circumstances, special effort is required.

This last point raises two exceedingly important questions: first, can this be done without the irreducible use of the rhetorical devices of simile, analogy and – most especially – metaphor in the case of everyday deployment of vague and general concepts and their introducing terms, and second, can technical precisification for special purposes (compass points, colour codes), requiring as it does definitional stipulations, or the construction of specialist vocabularies as with mathematics and fundamental science, be enough to provide a perspicuous and remainderless explanatory rendering of the concepts there deployed (equivalently: translation of the terms introducing them) in everyday (classical) terms?

The point about metaphor is of such importance in answering these questions that it is discussed at more length below (§5).

If attention is turned, however, from the problem of the border – or the borderlessness – infecting the region where such terms as 'red' and 'orange' abut, to *users* of these terms, and concentrate on what is arguably the more significant question of what would count as competency in their practice, we note that it is displayed by the conjunction of three things: the ability to identify focal cases of each, the ability to identify focal cases where neither applies (variations of green as opposed to black, etc.), and the same general hesitancy as displayed by other users when the terms cease to apply unqualifiedly. The absence of determinate conditions for application of the terms is no barrier to their usefulness, instead is a component of their usefulness, for when phenomena lack hard edges while displaying clarity in focal and contrasting cases, language apt for successful communication about them accommodates to that fact. The phenomena in the case of colours are visually experienced surfaces, and their indicative samples are ostensively defined; but in many if not most other cases they are concepts – vague and general concepts.

Nevertheless the colour example affords useful purchase in thinking about these latter. Much attention has been applied to the search for necessary and sufficient conditions for something to fall into the extension of a general term, or to supervaluational and subvaluational theories of the truth-conditions of predications of vague terms in their problematic border regions of application (familiarly exemplified by 'bald' and 'heap'). Here the focus is on the *terms*, and by extension the properties or collections of items they refer to, rather than the use made of them by competent speakers, where, as in the colour case, it is no barrier to effective use that vague terms have fuzzy borders of application and that crisp criteria for membership of the extensions of general terms are absent. On the contrary, competent uses of both vague and general terms do not require that the properties they denote or classes they delineate have sharp limits so that statements predicating the terms can have definite truth-values. Instead it would appear not merely natural but arguably appropriate that such terms should figure in judgments regarded as *roughly true* or (not very differently) as entailing speakers' acceptance of the notion of degrees of truth; more conservative though still revisionary is the suggestion that the problem is best addressed by postulating truth-values additional to 'true' and 'false'; less conservatively one might try the idea that truth is structured and has 'parts' which can be invoked to account for the fuzziness of the terms' application (or of the sets of entities to which they refer).[16]

Some of the implications of such suggestions can seem promising; Łukasiewicz's suggestion about a third truth-value, viz. 'possible', or technical specifications of assignments to fuzzy sets, open the way to alternative approaches, though in the debate about them the idea that many-valued propositional logics can be shown to have a bivalent semantics (the 'Suszko Reduction') has to be countered in any version exported to the natural language case, for example in trying to make intuitive sense of 'possible' as a third value which is not just ellipsis for 'possibly true'. But the fact is that formal treatments of the logical requirements for the semantics of the kind of expressions at issue almost comprehensively miss their *point* (in the 'sense-force-point' sense of 'point' – viz. speakers' intentions and the collaboration of these with hearers' expected interpretations). For example: it is hard not to see the subvaluational or dialetheist approach (in which, in 180° contrast to supervaluation's truth-value gaps, there is truth-value abundance, in the sense that a statement can be both true and false, paraconsistently viewed) as forcing an issue which by its nature resists such forcing. This approach is a semantic near-equivalent of differential calculus; saying (p_1) 'it is true that q (that x is a *heap* of sand when n grains are present)' under one precisification of the assertion is like deriving the slope of the line tangent at one point on a curve, while saying (p_2) 'it is false that q' under another precisification of the assertion is like deriving a different value for the slope at a

---

[16]In the offing, J. L. Austen on 'roughly true' variously and frequently implied, *Philosophical Papers*, 3rd edn., J. O. Urmson and G. J. Warnock (eds.) (Oxford University Press 1979); Frege on 'parts' of truth 1892, 'Über Sinn und Bedeutung', *Zeitschrift für Philosophie und philosophische Kritik* 100: 25–50 (Reprinted in B. McGuinness (ed.), *Collected Papers on Mathematics, Logic, and Philosophy*, Blackwell 1984.)

different point – and then pointing out that the conjunction '(p_1 & p_2) is true' is analogous to the same curve necessarily yielding (*qua* curve) different derivatives at different points. Although the analogy is itself forced, it comes closest when saying 'dy/dx as x approaches zero allows treating the curve as a straight line', for this does the work of treating the predication of a vague property as having a determinate truth value under some possible precisification, even if in practice the precisification cannot be effected.

The objection to this is that it misses the essential point of vague expressions, which is to dispense with possible precisifications altogether; that is precisely their informational value. Their point lies in their use, and mastery of them requires evaluation in terms of communicative success or appropriateness, such that when this is achieved utterances in which they are predicated informally merit description by the placeholder '__is true'. If a speaker insisted on (say) a trichologically exact specification of the maximum number of hairs on a head beyond which a predication of '__is bald' is illegitimate, they would be manifesting an at least distorted grasp of 'bald', since that would mark a point at which the addition of a single hair switches the truth-value – and 'splitting hairs' is what vague expressions are designed to avoid.

The scheme, thus, requires irreducibly vague expressions, and in doing so again manifests its ad hoc nature. For creatures existing at the scale of human beings it would be surprising to find that compromises over how the phenomena are to be described are unnecessary. To concentrate upon the utility of vague expressions for communication is to recognise a further feature of the way evaluative concepts work in the scheme: in the case of vagueness the substituends for '_is true' include '_is appropriate', '_is informative', '_is successful'. Consider a case where you are asked to deliver a message to someone you do not know, and he is described as 'young, tall, thin and bald' so that you can pick him out, and by their means you do indeed pick him out; despite all these terms being vague their use has been informative and successful, and on returning to the message-sender you might well therefore say, 'What you said of him is true', meaning that thus describing him *worked*: it enabled identification. Although there are doubtless exact precisifications of the identifying information that could be provided in this case ('He is twenty three years four months and fifteen days old, six feet three and three quarter inches tall, has one hundred and eighty two hairs on his scalp ... ') their being otiose, or time-consuming, or over-exact (misidentification might result if the would-be identifient had worn shoes with higher heels that day and was therefore not exactly six feet three and three quarter inches in height on being encountered), would undermine the communicative utility achieved by employment of vague expressions. But note that this is a case where precisification is achieved by invoking what lies on the focal side of a term's application; being six feet three inches in height is tall by any standards. The messenger's problem would arise if he were five feet eleven and a half inches in height, say, or twenty-eight years old, or better described as 'lean' or 'slender' instead of 'thin'. This makes 'tall', 'thin' and the rest like 'red': *essentially* without precisifiable borders unless by stipulation.

An alternative take on this point is provided by addressing the issue as one conceived in terms of how semantic indeterminacy is to be managed if one's commitment is to a determinate bivalent conception of truth as central to semantics. Viewed thus, the foregoing argument has it that we implicitly commit ourselves to *not being able to say* what the truth value is in borderline cases, and that this is a crucial feature of the usefulness of vague expressions. Doing so does not by itself entail that the expressions definitely lack a truth value, for those whose commitment to determinate truth is non-negotiable; the weight of the point bears on the utility of 'not being able to say' –

paradoxical as it might seem to invoke this as essential to achieving communicative success.[17]

But this might be to concede too much to semantic truth-realists. A suggestion arises here: the metrics of evaluation of discourses in which semantic indeterminacy occurs get into trouble when the only options considered are truth-conditions. Such evaluations of discourse as their being rhetorically effective, mellifluously spoken, elegantly written, and the like, are philosophically unimportant; but it is far from philosophically unimportant whether the discourse succeeds in its primary purpose of communicating, and here the requirement that it can only do so if it has not only a truth-value but a determinable one runs into immediate difficulty. For one (familiar) thing, the truth-conditions of many statements are recognition-transcendent, and many of these many are not merely indeterminable in practice but in principle (e.g. some statements about the past), so the consequence for subvaluational approaches to vagueness is to say that there is therefore a determinately true or false answer to the question, 'If I take away one more hair, is he bald?' which is opposite in truth value to the immediately preceding token of that question, but that we cannot in principle know which pair of answers this is. But if one introduces semantic indeterminacy as a property ascribable *in evaluations* of discourses, properly recognised as a crucial component in the work done by vague expressions, then the menu of options extends beyond 'truth-value gaps' or 'determinate but in principle indeterminable truth value' to 'intrinsically semantically indeterminate' itself. And this in turn suggests that the idea to be developed is that in these cases – remembering that they are very numerous, and run throughout the fabric of almost all (other than

---

[17]Grayling, 'Publicity, Stability and "Knowing the Meaning"' in *Truth, Meaning and Realism* 2007.

stipulatively precise, as in mathematics) discourses – the evaluation to be made is not 'is true' ('is false') but 'is correct (or appropriate) usage' ('is incorrect/inappropriate usage').

The temptation to think that the concept of 'correctness' itself is parasitic on truth ('the usage is correct or appropriate if it says something true') is quickly resisted when noticing that evaluations of statements of other forces (interrogative, imperative, optative) as appropriate when occurring in some stretch of discourse are independent of the role of truth in individuating forces ('Is it true?' 'Make it true!' 'I wish it were true' etc.) Asking a question – 'asking *that* question' – can be appropriate or inappropriate independently of the fact that to ask a question is to ask whether such and such is the case. Likewise, even truth-evaluable utterances can be appropriate or their use correct independently of their truth-value. It is appropriate to say such things as 'Nice to meet you', 'That was delicious', when neither is true. Consider shared hesitancies over whether 'red' applies to a particular colour; not identifying it as definitely red or definitely not red is appropriate, and conveys what might be significant information; disagreement over whether someone is or is not bald does not impugn the disputants' general understanding of 'bald' but is an expected property of the semantics of the term itself which explains why the contrasting idiolectic choices of whether or not to apply it in the given case results in disagreement. In the offing of this approach is what has been called 'contextualism'; the emphasis here is on the context of use, but where considerations of use in the given context are the dominant factor.[18]

The essential fuzziness of the borders of vague terms and the concepts they introduce is more than a hint that the domain of their

---

[18]Hans Kamp, 'The Paradox of the Heap' (1981), in Uwe Münnich (ed.) *Aspects of Philosophical Logic* (Cambridge University Press, 1996) 225–77.

application is artefactual; it is variably carved according to interest, not according to putative joints existing interest-independently. This prompts one to examine concepts introduced by general terms or sortals, terms for natural and artificial kinds, and the questions of identity and essence that arise in connection with them. A route through this extensive terrain of debate is indicated by the discussion of vagueness. (See §6's discussion of concept reference.)

Whatever else one thinks about Locke's philosophy of language, it is hard to disagree with his remarks in the *Essay* III.iii 'Of General Terms', 'The greatest part of words are general terms' and 'General and universal are creatures of the understanding, and belong not to the real existence of things', a point reinforced, not refuted, by Berkeley's rejection in the 'Introduction' to the *Principles* of Locke's account of abstract ideas as the denotata of general terms, given Berkeley's own better account of such concepts as collecting particulars any one of which can stand as a representative instance of the concept's application.[19]

---

[19]Cf. Grayling, *Berkeley*.

§4

Truth and Assertion

There are, familiarly, two general approaches to truth. One says that it is a substantive property of whatever the truth-bearers are (statements, propositions, theories), either a relational property such as correspondence or coherence, or a functional property such as epistemic utility as in the pragmatic theory. An outlier in this approach is the view that truth is a substantive but indefinable property, a tack taken by Donald Davidson.[1] The other is the deflationary approach, which takes a number of forms such as redundancy, minimalism, prosententialism and disquotationalism. A generic characterisation of deflationism is that if the notion of truth is not actually empty there is anyway nothing more to it than use of the predicate '__is true' as a convenience for certain logical, grammatical and rhetorical purposes.

The view on offer in what follows says that truth is a substantive property, indeed is not one but a number of substantive properties, introduced *via* a family of cognitively significant notions. Among the benefits of this approach is that it illuminates both what is right and wrong with traditional theories of substantive truth, and illustrates

---

[1] Donald Davidson, 'Reality Without Reference', 'A Coherence Theory of Truth and Knowledge' in E. Lepore (ed.) *Truth and Interpretation* (Blackwell 1986); 'The Folly of Trying to Define Truth' *Journal of Philosophy* Vol. XCIII (1996).

why Ramsey is right to say that the important task is to formulate a theory of assertion.[2]

Accepting this point from Ramsey is not to concede anything to deflationism beyond agreeing that it is clearly right in many cases of saying 'that's true' or 'it is true that__' that we are just marking agreement or emphasising, and also that '__is true' effectively avoids iteration of whatever is agreed with, obviating the need to reassert whole theories or long chains of conjunctions and disjunctions. But consider what deflationists say in response to the challenge that *truth matters* – in a court of law, in scientific enquiry, in identifying the location of enemy forces – namely, that the work done by '__is true' is already done by the utterance to which this predicate is applied. That this is at least questionable is suggested by this: if I say, 'I've put a million dollars in your bank account' and you ask, doubtless in tones of disbelief, 'Is that true?' and I reply, 'What does it add to attach a truth-value to what I've just said?' you might feel that this will not quite do, unless the speech-act of assertion *just as such* automatically guarantees itself ('as true' we are ineluctably tempted to say) – which cannot be right, given the defeasibility of all assertions about contingent matters. Nevertheless the deflationist is not without recourse in responding to the 'truth matters' challenge, and what she might say will be of interest in what follows.

A further preliminary is required, concerning truth-bearers, sentences, non-trivial spatio-temporally indexed utterances of declarative sentences (making statements; asserting) and propositions, as follows.

The question of what truth-bearers are is treated as a straightforward aspect of the view offered here; it says that two kinds of thing are

---

[2]Frank P. Ramsey, 'Facts and Propositions' (1927), reprinted in *F.P. Ramsey: Philosophical Papers*, ed. D. H. Mellor (Cambridge University Press 1990) 34–51.

standard examples of truth-bearers: *theories*, and the *phrastics of utterances*, phrastics being what constitute the truth-evaluable components of utterances. I put matters this way so that a theory of force is straightforwardly available on the view being described here (assertoric force just is the phrastic, the interrogative is 'Is the [phrastic] … ?', the imperative is 'Make it be that the [phrastic] … !', the optative 'I wish that the [phrastic] … '). How a phrastic is expressed is to be represented propositionally, in the form *that p* as in a locution such as 'it is true *that 1+1 = 2 in arithmetic to base 10*'. But conveniently, as a *façon de parler*, one can say '"s" is true' where 's' is either an eternal sentence or a sentence of the language uttered non-trivially, on an occasion, in declarative mode, to make a statement. (To 'make a statement that p' with the perlocutionary intentions described below as constitutive of asserting is, therefore, to *assert* p: more below.) So in the following, examples 1 and 3 are taken as respectively equivalent in their predicative form to 2 and 4:

1 '1+1=2' is true.

2 'it is true *that 1+1=2*'.

3 'Everest is the highest mountain' (as non-trivially uttered by someone in the present geological epoch) is true.

4 'it is true *that Everest is the highest mountain* (as non-trivially uttered by someone in the present geological epoch).

Examples 1 and 2 are eternal sentences, and require no indexing to a speaker and occasion; they may be regarded as *standing statements*. In 3 the property of being true is predicated of the *statement* made by use of the sentence 'Everest is the highest mountain' on an occasion; in 4 the property of being true is, again on an occasion, predicated of the *proposition* denoted by *that Everest is the highest mountain*. This taxonomy commits one to the view that propositions are what sentences express – or equivalently but better, that sentences are names of propositions and therefore, when non-trivially uttered by a speaker on an occasion to make a statement, refer to the proposition. This is intuitive, for the point could be expanded to involve considerations about what a speaker intends to convey and what thought is being picked out by the given utterance, in all cases requiring that *that p* be the *content* onto which all such trajectories of identifying *what is said, what is meant, what is conveyed* converge.[3]

While this tack offers a convenient way of characterising synonymity and benchmarks for reducing opacity in radical translation by providing a target for translators to aim at, it also raises the question whether it invites a difficulty in intensional contexts. A suggestion that effectively parks the concern is that the failure of intersubsitutivity *salva veritate* of the *sentences* 'Cicero wrote *On Duties*' and 'Tully wrote *On Duties*' as names of the proposition *that Marcus Tullius Cicero wrote On Duties* in the context 'John believes that Cicero wrote *On Duties*' but does not know that Cicero and Tully are the same person, is a function of the ignorance-induced failure of the intersubsitutivity *salva veritate* of the *names* 'Cicero' and 'Tully'; compositionality goes all the way down as well as up.

In saying that propositions represent the phrastic component of utterances of different forces, and that statements are sentences used on particular occasions to refer to propositions, no realist entailment follows to propositions being abstract entities existing independently of occasions of non-trivial utterance of sentences.[4] A nominalistic

---

[3]Although for the sake of precision the distinction between a sentence – a grammatically well-formed string of words in a given natural language (the correlative term is 'formula' for a formal language) – and a statement as a non-trivial indexically-particular *use* of a sentence, no harm is done if unqualified uses of 'sentence' are understood, by context, as doing duty for the latter.

[4]Eternal sentences are such because they *stand ready* for use *on any occasion* and require no indices of utterance. They are, in effect, always in utterance.

account is sufficient, in which propositions are what is expressed in common by all sentences whose use is intended to convey them, for example 'snow is white', 'xue shi baide', 'neige est blanche', 'Schnee ist weiss', 'aggregations of atmospherically-formed and precipitated ice-crystals reflect all visible wavelengths of light', etc. This is of course the entrance to a rabbit-hole, because 'a proposition is what is expressed by all sentences whose use is intended to convey it' is circular and reinvites the matter of 'meanings' and 'sets of synonymous sentences' suggested in the previous paragraph to be illuminated, not exacerbated, by the approach – yet now their reappearance in this more committal guise threatens exacerbation, or at least to defer a solution rather than provide one. Well, yes; the account is circular; but the circle is a virtuous one, as a rephrasing shows: *that snow is white* is what utterers of 'snow is white', 'xue shi baide', 'neige est blanche' etc. all intend to assert; the conceptual weight is transferred to speakers' communicative aims and the *use* made of the sentences in question to achieve them. And use is where 'the spade is turned'. If one ventures any further down the rabbit-hole, one will find oneself playing there the game aptly described by Dennett as 'Anything you can do I can do meta'.[5]

And so to the main event. On the view offered here, to say 'Truth is a number of substantive properties' is to say in the material mode what in the linguistic mode is said by 'The predicate "__is true" is a placeholder for more explicit predicates of positive epistemic evaluation (in the case of "__is false" of negative evaluation) individuated by discourse' – as shown by the fact that answers to the

---

[5] I acknowledge the triple mixing of metaphors here (spade rabbit-hole game) – reminiscent of the famous case of Sir Boyle Roche's epic 'Mr Speaker, I smell a rat; I see him forming in the air, but I'll nip him in the bud' – but as later remarks show, metaphor is not only extremely useful in explanation and clarification, but in key cases irreducible. It is not irreducible in this case, just clarificatory.

question, 'What are candidate substituends for "__is true"?' depends on the discourse in which the predication is made.

For example: in predications of '_is true' to

1   1+1=2

2   There is a glass of water on the table

3   Lying is wrong

4   Quarks cannot exist singly

what is meant, when cashed out more explicitly, in each case is different. Candidates (just as examples) are:

a   '__is constructible';

b   '__is perceptually verifiable';

c   '__is desirable to believe and act upon';

d   '__is entailed by the theory of the strong nuclear force'.

The predications in a – b look straightforwardly to be examples of *assertibility*. There is much right but something wrong about this appearance. Recall that 'assertibility' was originally proposed as a weaker but more realistic alternative to 'truth' on the grounds that an utterer might be in the best possible position to assert p even when p is false – so the epistemic fact of defeasibility, a universal characteristic of the realms of contingency, is accommodated by weakening the best evaluation that we can give an utterance. On this view assertibility does not *replace* truth but itself requires to be defined in terms of it, thus: 'S has the best available grounds for asserting "p" but p is false'. But if so, 'assertible' is the wrong substituend for a, b and perhaps d, because instead of explaining *what work a predicate of positive epistemic evaluation is doing* it is simply, and question-beggingly, moving what is meant by 'truth' *qua* 'something more than assertibility' one stage further off.

What is right about the appearance, however, is that if predicating truth actually *consists in* 'asserting under government of the discourse's epistemic constraints', then we see the weight of the matter lying on the concept of 'the work done by a predicate of positive epistemic evaluation'.[6] And we see this *via* recognising the illocutionary and especially perlocutionary forces of assertion, as follows.

When one asserts a proposition, one is laying claim to its possessing at least these seven properties: that it is reliable in inference, that it is consistent with other propositions we likewise value, that it is usable in evaluating other propositions, that it invites agreement, that it is epistemically authoritative for us in the given domain of discourse, that accepting it is a norm for rationality, and that it does or can play a role in helping us to organise the subject-matter in question more effectively – 'effectively' by the epistemic standards applied in the evaluation – than competitors to it. The *point* of asserting is to recommend or prescribe agreement and the consequences of agreement.

One can collect and summarise these properties under higher-order headings relating to their fulfilment of desiderata of acceptability, utility, adequacy and stability in assertoric practice. *Acceptability* relates to assertions' solicitation of acceptance on the basis of negotiated ways of maximising agreement by triangulation on evidence, aims and context of utterance. *Utility* relates to assertions' provision of information, generation of predictions, licensing of inferences, and settling disputes through agreement when the latter is achieved. *Adequacy* relates to the fittingness or appropriateness of an

---

[6]Even in the moral case the evaluation in question is epistemic, in the sense that it involves knowing when the utterance is justified and what justifies it.

assertion to fulfilling the desiderata of acceptability and utility, while *stability* concerns the way assertions serve as constituents of a view of the given domain that is cogent, consistent, and robust in tests and other demands upon it, thus counting as 'facts' in the domain. This list is redundant, in that the desiderata obviously overlap and combine, but it is useful to distinguish the aspects in this way because in taking for granted what work is done by accepting propositions as true we overlook the practicalities of what such acceptance entails, *these* being what give the concept its content in various discourses.

What by symmetry we must describe as 'disvalued' propositions are those that fail to exhibit these features, though they can, and often do, seem to exhibit them until they fail under one or another kind of test. In this respect what is right in the pragmatists' theory of truth – that the true is what is useful to believe (better: to accept and apply) – gets some support, given that what is taken to be true because it cashes out in experience can turn out to be no longer useful to hold as enquiry proceeds. In ordinary parlance disvalued propositions are labelled 'false' but it would be more accurate to label them 'not true' to mark the fact that there is more than one way they can fail to be true (by being meaningless, or neither true nor false, or inappropriate to the domain as e.g. in the case of category mistakes, which make them 'not even false').

We speak of information being conveyed by true propositions. This feature of propositions' utility and stability, when achieved, is allied to the notion of fact. The chief advantage of facts is their use in serving as premises for further inferences, and as the basis for rational action. One way to redescribe the concept of a fact is to say it is what is denoted by an assertion that stands firm for the domain in the ways described. In the traditional correspondence theory a duality of fact and proposition is required for there to be a relation which, when it exists, gives the content of '__is true'. On the view taken here, differently, an aspect of the identity theory of truth is satisfied: facts are ('are' here the copula of identity) assertions that stand firm for the domain.

Notice a nuance here. Assertions are 'propositions offered on an occasion in a discourse as candidates for premises, bases for action, etc.', that is, they are not *just* 'offered propositions' (and certainly not *just* propositions). So the old way (so to say) of putting matters, viz. 'facts are true propositions', is here superseded by 'facts are accepted assertions'. There is more to this difference than meets the eye: the circumstances of utterances and their intended and actual reception figure in the account of the broad context to which essential reference is necessary. (Bear in mind that in the argument of this book invocation of the concept of broad context is indispensable to understanding reference; since reference is taken to be discourse-relative the ontology projected by the discourse constitutes the required context, and this determines choice of a theory of reference – given that e.g. rigidity and causal theories are predicated on one model of what such a context can be – the spatio-temporal model – it is evident why, when it turns out that this model has to be assimilated to a general projectivist model, a theory of reference via sense becomes irresistible.)

Since so much is made of the concept of evaluation in this account – to repeat: '__is true' is a placeholder predicate for predicates of positive *evaluation* of assertions in a domain such as '__is constructible', '__is empirically verifiable', etc. – it is helpful to pause for a moment to inspect it. Consider analogous cases: what are the judges in sheepdog trials looking for? There are criteria of evaluation for how effectively sheepdogs serve their purposes, embracing the connected matters of their behaviour and temperament: they need to be docile to command, to be nigh indefatigable, to marshal sheep neatly without injuring them, and so on. A musician considering whether to purchase a violin will evaluate it on different criteria: playability, tone, the security of the pegs and bridge, the fitness of the chinrest and fingerboard to her manner of playing. In both cases, a judgment is being made about what value to place on something (in some cases in money terms, in others in epistemic terms, in yet others, when this is different, in terms of practical utility). What we apply the generic '__is true' to in any given discourse is what meets the criteria for application of the more particular predicate expressing a positive judgment – an evaluation – licensing it as a basis for inference and action (etc.) as above. And this thereby is to specify the content of '__is true' (of 'truth') in general.

Ramsey's view that what we require in place of a theory of truth is a theory of assertion rests on the observation that assertion is and does everything that talk of truth is shorthand for. What the foregoing suggests is that in demonstrating that assertibility exhausts truth (more circumstantially: that assertibility-in-a-domain exhausts the concept of truth-for-that-domain) turns on specifying in particular the *perlocutionary* aim of asserting, which (to repeat) is to license the content of the assertion as a premise for further reasoning, a justification for acting, a security for a bet, a keying of a region of discourse, and an invitation and recommendation for anyone who understands the assertion to think and act likewise.[7] This in turn is to say that there are, literally, different kinds of truth.

---

[7]At this point the debate about Wittgenstein's remark in *Philosophical Investigations* §22, based on his disagreement with Frege's account of the dual nature of assertoric utterances as involving both a *judgment* about a thought and *saying that* it is true, comes to mind. Wittgenstein held that Frege's judgment stroke is 'logically meaningless' (*Notebook* 1913: 95) on the grounds that assertion is 'merely psychological'; in *PI* the apparent point (described by Dummett as 'confused') is that the nature of assertion entails a redundancy view of truth. On the view here the claim is that to assert is to *display* the propositional attitude ('judging that', 'taking it that') just as asking a question *displays that* it is a question and implies that the questioner does not know the answer.

Tarski suspected that this might be the case.[8] In line with his hint, this explains why 'truth' in formal contexts has to be considered separately, treating talk of the semantics of formal languages as metaphorical, such that talk of 'truth' or 'constructability' and like variants for such a language is a metalinguistic description of a syntactic property, arguably (on some views) the only kind of property that such languages have.

But the agreement with Ramsey that a theory of assertion should replace a theory of truth does not constitute agreement with his reason for thinking so. The view here urged resists the deflationary claim that it is a misconception to think that there is a property denoted by 'truth' with explanatory structure, saying by sharp contrast that there is a number of such properties, the introducing predicates for which '__is true' holds a place.

We can now notice a further point, relating to why it is that the generic placeholder '__is true' can do duty for all the discourse-relative predicates. It is because what it picks out is that a positive evaluation (as inference-licensing etc.) is in play. Consider how, for reasons of brevity and facility of communication, natural language makes use of many placeholder predicates. Consider '__is good' and '__is beautiful'. A good dinner, a good dog, a good knife, a good book, a good pair of shoes, all require something more explanatory as a substitute for 'good' if justification for the claim is demanded. And so likewise for a beautiful sunset, face, melody, ballet performance, summer.

'True' (and likewise 'good' and 'beautiful' – and likewise again 'false', 'bad', 'ugly') is what might be called a 'generic term' or even a 'metaterm'.

---

[8]Alfred Tarski, 'The Concept of Truth in Formalized Languages' in J. H. Woodger, *Logic, Semantics, Metamathematics* (Oxford University Press 1956) 152–278, and see 'The Semantic Conception of Truth' in H. Feigl and W. Sellars, *Readings in Philosophical Analysis* (Appleton-Century-Crofts 1949) 52–84.

It is a shorthand; such terms occupy a metalevel with respect to the families of more specific and defined expressions for which they do duty. Natural languages are replete with metaterms: 'thing' (noun), 'nice' (positive adjective), are undoubtedly the commonest examples. They constitute an important class of expressions, not only from the point of view of their role in communicative success, but because they have been fruitful in philosophical confusion, one main reason being the assumption that they have a *nongeneric* univocal meaning and (if this is different) single use because they do indeed *generically* have such a meaning and use. The generic univocality of 'true' lies in its use to mark that an utterance carries a positive epistemic evaluation in whatever discourse it is applied in; the discourse-*local* predicate carries the explanatory and logical weight, which '__is true' derives from it by courtesy. That is just what we mean by committing ourselves to an utterance's *being true* even in the shadow of defeasibility; to characterise it as generic says how 'true' works as a shorthand in contingent cases.

And it is as a generic that 'true' operates in inferences, in the explanation of validity in terms of truth-preservingness. Soundness, by contrast, always turns on the more particular discourse-relative property for which '__is true' does duty. It is a virtue of the approach here that, e.g., an ethical non-cognitivist thereby has an account of a way ethical utterances can be ascribed the property for which '__ is true' holds a place, by using the generic term to demonstrate the validity of such inferences as:

It is true that stealing is wrong.
If it is true that stealing is wrong, people should be encouraged not
   to steal.
Therefore, it is true that people should be encouraged not to steal.

Arguably, it is a key function of generic 'true' to allow that the forms of inferences can be displayed across discourses, and explains the different roles of the concepts of validity and soundness in inference. Generic 'true' is enough for the discourse-independent concepts of form and validity; in contrast, soundness is contingent on the discourse-relative content of utterances and the means in that discourse of ascertaining whether they satisfy the requirements for assertibility.

The standard view of the concept of assertion is that it not only 'essentially engages' with the concept of truth but depends for its content on a prior grasp of an independently-specified concept of truth.[9] The view being urged here is that matters are the other way round; that it is assertion that explains truth. But there is still more to say in support of this contention, as follows.

Certain further preliminaries require notice. One involves addressing the idea that, and if so in what sense, assertion is 'fact-stating discourse'.[10] On standard views in which understanding assertion is made to depend on some antecedently defined substantive and univocal notion of truth, the mutual relationship of 'truth' and 'fact' (as in 'a fact is a true proposition') prompts the concern that the account is question-begging. Even if this anxiety were quelled, however, it will still not do to define assertion as fact-stating discourse, because some assertions are false, and *ipso facto* do not state facts. So even on this view fact stating is, at best, something that only true assertions do, and therefore if the stating of facts is to figure centrally

---

[9] Cf. C. Wright, 'Realism, Antirealism, Irrealism, Quasi-Realism' in P. A. French et al., *Midwest Studies in Philosophy XII: Realism and Antirealism* (University of Minnesota Press 1988) p. 25 et. seq.

[10] This is the view taken by P. F. Strawson and Huw Price. P. F. Strawson, 'Truth' in *Logico-Linguistic Papers* (Methuen 1971); H. Price, 'Truth and the Nature of Assertion' *Mind* 86(382) (1987): 202–220 and in *Facts and the Function of Truth* (Oxford University Press 1988) esp. pp. 9–13.

in the account, it would have to be as what an asserter intends to do, not what she invariably does. But she only succeeds in her intention when certain conditions are fulfilled, which is just where, on the standard account, the notion of truth is brought in. Suppose this is done (as it is typically done in such accounts) by saying that the essential condition is that the content of the assertion corresponds to an independently-existing states of affairs. This is to take as the model the simplest case, viz. assertions about states of affairs (or some preferred alternative) in an empirically-accessible environment. But this is questionable in the case of e.g. mathematical and ethical assertions, inviting considerable complication over the status of the distal relata; which, once one recognises this as precisely the difficulty caused by treating '__is true' univocally for *all* discourses, prompts one to consider 'fact' as a metaterm for 'accepted assertion' and therefore as coterminous with, if not a synonym of, 'truth' in *its* metatermic sense. And this reverses the explanatory dependence of 'fact-stating' and 'assertion'; the latter is not explained by saying that it is the former, but the former is explained as what is constituted by a paradigmatic state of the latter (the state of being accepted for reliable use in inference, etc.) in a discourse.

A more substantial point is raised by noting that when some S asserts p in the standard case, S's act of asserting *expresses* S's commitment to p's possessing the properties described above. But an expressivist reading of the act should not mislead one into thinking (as expressivism does in ethical theory, e.g.) that no more is involved than S's giving vent to a personal attitude. The idea that it indeed involves no more than this seems to be naturally implied by views in which the ontology of the domain of discourse in the context of which p is asserted is conceived antirealistically, for the precise reason that p's content does not latch on to anything independent of it.

A sceptic about such a view might therefore feel entitled to claim that S is accordingly 'not really asserting' but (as it were) only mimicking assertion. What is it to 'mimic assertion'? The suggestion is that S is ('only', 'just') 'saying that' p, borrowed from the case of reported utterances and other indirect contexts. But the class of 'sayings that' is larger than the class of assertions, as shown by considering deceiving and lying, in which S says that p in order to mislead her audience. In purposing to deceive, S pretends to assert (to be committed to possession by p of the properties described above) but does not in fact do so: if S pretends to assert p, S is not asserting p. But she is saying that p. So asserting is at most a subset of sayings-that.

An objector at this point might argue that distinguishing asserting from saying-that positively cries out for an antecedent notion of truth, because the analysis of the situation in which S says that p in order to mimic asserting p is that S attempts to get her audience to accept as true what she knows to be false, and *this* is precisely why her utterance is only a pretend-assertion – thus appearing to demonstrate the nature of the interdependence of truth and assertion in which the former is separate and prior. But to argue thus is simply to miss out the crucial next step, to asking 'What in normal cases is S aiming at in asserting p?', the answer being: assuring interlocutors that they can 'rely on, premise, trust, etc., p in the discourse'. Since this is the whole substance of assertion, with the reliance, trust, etc. cashing out in different ways in different discourses, the error lies in taking the convenience of having the shorthand '__is true' to predicate of p and converting it into an antecedently-specified and univocally understood property of any saying-that in any discourse that is to pass muster as an assertion. This is akin to a form of hypostatisation, giving a denotation to a metaterm, which in the analogous case of '__ is good' would immediately be seen (by anyone other than a die-hard

Platonist) implausibly to entail that the 'good' in 'good government', 'good shoes', 'good dinner' is all the same 'goodness'.

Assertion is indeed expression of an epistemic attitude, but the 'more' that makes it 'more than merely' expression is the cashable consequence of accepting what is asserted. On this view assertion is, as noted, the conjunction of an expression of a complex attitude on the asserter's part and an implied prescriptive element placing or seeking to place on her audience the normativity and 'rational command' obligations which in the shorthand vocabulary of truth-talk we describe as respect for and epistemic submission to truth.[11] The attitude expresses S's conceptual commitments, having which – under the authority of the way they are acquired – puts them into a disciplined relation of engagement with responsible reasoning and action elsewhere in S's epistemic concerns, and more broadly with her commitment to her epistemic community. This latter centrally includes what in Bernard Williams's terms would be described as a truthfulness obligation; in the idiom of the theory here, an apt formulation would be 'certification to the epistemic community, in and by the very act of asserting, that the content of the assertion is epistemically reliable'.[12] This is what makes it non-arbitrary, and the domain of the discourse a realm of actual and possible fact.

We see this by noting that when S asserts p, thereby expressing (explicitly manifesting) commitment to the reliability of p (as a premise in further inference, etc.), acceptance of its content by her audience is a move in the constitution of facticity, in the sense that what counts as 'the facts' in a domain of discourse is constituted by agreements, reached under the discipline of the constraints on

---

[11]A host of associations arise here: cf. Bernard Williams, *Truth and Truthfulness* (Princeton University Press 2004). Carnap was among the first to note the prescriptive element in assertion.

[12]Bernard Williams, *ibid.*

enquiry in that domain, among discoursers. Given the defeasibility of assertions about contingent matters, the aspiration of assertions to convey facts and their taking the form of doing so, it is more modestly rendered as *proposing* fact, the making of a move in the negotiation over what is to count as factual. This in turn is done by achieving consensus among discoursers over given sets of assertions.

The spectre of an unpalatable kind of relativistic irrealism that this remark conjures up is held at bay by noticing that acts of assertion and their reception (acceptance or rejection) by their audience, where both the assertion and the audience's evaluation of it are supported by reasons that claim rational respect, are controlled by the canons of enquiry for the domain. A simple example is an assertion made in discoursing about medium-sized dry-goods in the perceptual environment: an assertion about some occurrent state of affairs nearby can be checked by looking. The procedures of acquiring and verifying information form a connected whole, while communicating it (by means of assertions) enacts, at least in aspiration, a certification that the procedures have been carried out. In linguistic mode the point can be put by saying that knowing what words mean involves knowing how to ascertain whether they apply in a given case – which is of course almost the whole of what it is to be a discourser. But the consideration generalises. To assert is to invite actual consequences in both cognitive and practical respects, and therefore has to lie under tough normative constraints, which include specification of tests for the right kinds of links between assertions and their grounds, for the adequacy of the grounds, and for the relevance of the acts of assertion to the circumstances of their making. As this suggests, irresponsible assertion – at one end of the spectrum claims made without sufficient justification, at the other end deliberate purveying of falsehoods, in which case it is 'pretended assertion' – is harmful to, even destructive of, the domain of discourse in which it occurs and thereby to the form of life constituted by the discourse. This is why a relativistic irrealism about the domain cannot stand up; the publicity and relative stability of meanings in the language of the discourse, without which communication is impossible, in embodying constraints on the use of its expressions, thereby say a great deal about what justifies an assertion if it is justified.[13]

The view taken here that truth is a number of different substantive properties of propositions, individuated by discourse, can stand alone, independently of theory to the effect that, in projecting the ontology of their domains, discourses render, as relative to themselves, the activities of referring to those domains and their contents and making assertions about them. But if a theory premised on this more general view is accepted, the discourse-relativity of truth understood as discourse-dependent varieties of assertibility follows naturally – one might say, directly. What has traditionally been regarded as the problem of truth is an artefact of the failure to see 'truth' (*mutatis* 'true', '___is true') as a metaerm, a generic placeholder, which tells us only one general thing across all discourses: that its substituends in those discourses are properties of positive epistemic value. By extension, seeking to give a univocal account of such terms ('good' and others) across discourses can be recognised as a fertile source of perplexity and mistake. I take it that this insight is a restatement of the view that philosophical perplexity arises from mistaken assimilations of one type of expression to another, or to univocalising, instead of recognising that they should be individuated according to their application in different discourses, which is done by paying attention to the work they do there. For they *are*, of course, what they *do*.

---

[13]Grayling, 'Publicity, Stability, and "Knowing the Meaning"' in *Truth, Meaning and Realism* 2007, 77–90.

§ 5

Metaphor

A case has been made for saying that metaphor has an irreducible role in discourses as underwriting the communicative, explanatory and organisational ambitions that are constitutive of them. This invites a general consideration of the nature of metaphor itself.[1]

Metaphor, simile and analogy play significant roles in enquiry and in making sense of the domains over which thought and enquiry range. They are not just a matter of utility but often indispensable to these practices. Metaphor, in particular, can be the heuristic that opens a path of enquiry, and is quite frequently the only handle we have on phenomena under scrutiny. When employed well it is instructive, explanatory and insight-bearing. It is remarkable how widely used it is as a tool of intellectual endeavour; it is present in, and is sometimes constitutive of, insights and understanding across the whole range of what human curiosity explores and creativity brings, from fundamental physics to art, mathematics and the social sciences.

At the same time metaphor carries, even more than simile and analogy, the risk of misdirection. If it is – to employ apt metaphors – a light that illuminates, it can also be an *ignus fatuus* that leads

---

[1] The following discussion was first published as the Introduction by Grayling to (ed.) Grayling and S. Wuppuluri, *Metaphors and Analogies in Sciences and Humanities* (Synthese Library Vol. 453) (Springer 2022).

astray across difficult terrains of thought. The question of how the misleading possibilities of metaphor are controlled is one that lies close to the most fundamental concerns of epistemology.

The following paragraphs raise some general points about the nature of metaphor, and introduce a suggestion about the logical character of the copula employed in metaphorical assertions which demarcates metaphor from simile and analogy, explains in part how metaphor can be – for all its illuminating power otherwise – a sometimes risky resource in enquiry, and suggests that there is an interesting task to be undertaken in understanding the cognitive mechanisms that make metaphor and the allied rhetorical device of metonymy work, mechanisms deeper than and different from those at work in similes and analogies.

Central to the cognitive processes of mind are pattern-seeking and sense-making, both interpretative acts. In both activities, closely linked as they are, the application of metaphors and similes has a significance close in importance to memory; one might have met with a thing or situation before, or with an instance of the kind of thing or situation, and memory will underwrite recognition, as this term itself implies: *re*cognition. But if one has not met with this thing or situation before, the next resource is to ask: what is it like? What can it be represented as, so that I can make sense of it? The first question seeks a simile as an answer, the second a metaphor. The resource of memory is present here too, in the case of simile recalling resembling features, in the case of metaphor summoning what can serve as an interpretative blueprint by means of a conceptual transfer of an interestingly deep kind. Calling these devices of thought 'figures of speech' is not inaccurate, but underplays the importance of their cognitive role; for standardly they are constitutive of the act of 'making sense' itself.

By conceptually revisualising something unfamiliar in terms of something familiar one domesticates it, so to speak; one provides conceptual house-room for it. It is heuristic in function, though whereas heuristics might provide a path into something further, metaphor is sometimes the end point of the sense-making enterprise; it is what our best current understanding of a domain consists in. This is the case with quantum theory which, at time of writing, admits of competing interpretations, some irreducibly metaphorical given the difficulty of translating quantum theoretical descriptions into a classical framework.

'Making sense' is the key idea in play. Using the terms 'target' and 'source' now familiar in conceptual metaphor theory – themselves metaphorical – to denote respectively the domain to be understood and the domain from which a means of making sense is drawn (so in 'all the world's a stage' the stage is the source, the world the target), one can list the functions of the source as: *describing, illuminating, illustrating, picturing, analogising, revealing,* and by these means *informing.* In this list appear functions also, and sometimes more directly, performed by similes and analogies, but the cognitive purpose of all three rhetorical devices is very close; compare 'My love is like a red, red rose' and 'Mary is the rose of Tralee'. In achieving the functions just listed, metaphor exploits the power of cognitive assimilation to transfer (consider the etymology of *meta*phor itself) from source to target what is to a sufficient *but figurative* degree *cognate, comparable, correspondent, homologous* or *parallel.* The qualifier *but figurative* is essential: there is no invariable suggestion that the source resembles (is 'like') the target in any literal respect. Rather, it is specifically intended that the source present the target under a description that is itself comprehensible and by its means makes the target comprehensible, or more so.

At the same time, employment of a metaphor is *not* an assertion that source and target are *related, kin, agnate, congeneric, allied* or *approximative,* or that the nature of the source is a *property* or *component* of the target. It is (or once was: it is now a cliché) illuminating and rhetorically effective to say, 'Life is a battle', but it is unilluminating and rhetorically clumsy to say 'A battle is a struggle' or 'War is a battle', which is what choice of something related, agnate, kin, and the rest, would give us. This point suggests that it might be part of the definition of metaphor that it expressly trades on *not* asserting likeness between target and source in any of *these* ways – the ways of surface similarity. For that, simile is precisely the tool.

If one puts together the insight that employment of a metaphor is intended to transfer intelligibility to the target from antecedent grasp of the source by using the relevant suggestive aspect of the source's illumination of the target, along with express recognition of the fact that literal identification is not intended, one sees that the copula 'is' in metaphorical statements has a unique logical character. It is neither the 'is' of identity nor the 'is' of predication. The 'is' in similes is, by contrast, a straightforward 'is' of predication. This is a logical difference between metaphors and similes which frequently makes no substantive difference, despite their rhetorical difference consisting in the fact that the asserted content trades empirically on literal resemblance in the one case and expressly not so in the other. But at times the difference is substantive, particularly when the employment of a metaphor is irreducible in the sense that no other way of making sense of the target is available.

To explain this more fully, compare the metaphorical with the identity-asserting and predicative cases, as follows.

The 'is' of identity asserts that what are putatively two or more are in fact one. In the case of a reduction of certain phenomena (say, intentional phenomena of psychology such as remembering and fearing) to another class (say, activitation of structures in the brain) without remainder, a strong claim might be intended to the effect that the identity is eliminative, or more weakly that the terms of the reduced and reducing classes can be intersubstituted *salva veritate* in extensional contexts (so they are coreferential, courtesy of the identity, even if differing in sense, as with 'the morning star' and the 'evening star' as designations of the planet Venus). Either way, the 'is' of identity says at least that if X and Y are identical all and only the properties of X are the properties of Y and vice versa. Obviously, that is not intended by employment of a metaphor.

The 'is' of predication states that the subject of a proposition has a certain property, or if the proposition has multiple subjects that they all have that property or stand in a specified relation to each other. 'Napoleon is short, Napoleon is a Corsican, Napoleon is a clever general' all tell us about properties of Napoleon. 'Napoleon is a whirlwind', said of him during his years of triumph, tells us about him (illuminates, reveals, informs) by doing something different: not by directly imputing a property to him, but by imputing *by implication* a property or properties that would make a man informatively describable as a whirlwind, and doing so by exploiting, in the proposition's logical form, the analogy with the 'is' of identity. Contrast this with 'Napoleon is like a whirlwind'; in this case – using a simile – the 'is' is indeed the 'is' of predication; the property of 'being like a whirlwind' is predicated of Napoleon. In the case of metaphor – 'Napoleon is a whirlwind' – what is explicitly at work is the non-literal use of the 'is' of identity, constituting for metaphor a logical category of the copula for itself and in this way defining 'metaphor' and distinguishing it from simile and analogy.

Similes and analogies differ too, in that whereas the former assert a likeness, an analogy asserts a comparison that is explicitly intended to be explanatory of its target. Thus, Janus-faced, it borrows something from both simile and metaphor. Some similes are analogies if they have expressly explanatory and not merely illustrative intent; some have just the latter. From the point of view of logical form, analogies can be expressed non-predicatively; Schrodinger's dead-and-alive cat is an analogy for superposed states, but the sense in which a cat's being both dead and alive is *like* superposed quantum states is not the same as the sense in which my love is *like* a red red rose. The cat case illustrates uncertainty, but the cat's existentially ambiguous condition is not *like* the psi-function of the system (cat, box, Geiger counter, gunpowder, etc.), whereas my love really is like a red red rose in respect of her efflorescent beauty. To capture the sense in which not all analogies are expressed in the form of similes, one notes that 'likeness' in a simile is always literal, the 'likeness' in an analogy is not always so and when not so is, in fact, metaphorical – it is not, note, the analogy itself which is metaphorical, but the imputation of 'likeness' between the analogy and its target. A toy cat is 'like' (looks like, resembles) a real cat; a cat that is both dead and alive simultaneously is 'like' (is an analogy for) a pre-interaction quantum state; the 'like' in the second case is a metaphorical 'like' that implies not actual resemblance but illustrative comparison.

It is worth repeating that the distinction between metaphor and the other two rhetorical devices is not cognitively significant, only rhetorically so, in case one thought that either a loss or a misdirection might follow, in relation to substantive content, from a choice of which figure to employ. All three devices have the primary sense-making, illuminative or illustrative function, but the question of which to use might be decided by any number of considerations – for example, Robbie Burns chose a simile to achieve an iambic tetrameter (first beat on the second word) in 'My *love* is *like* a *red*, red *rose*' but had he wished to write that poem in trochaic tetrameter (first beat on the first word) he would have written '*My* love *is* a *red*, red *rose*', thus choosing a metaphor. The *poetic* significance of the choice of metre makes the choice between simile and metaphor non-arbitrary, but one can think of many cases where using a simile in place of a metaphor or vice versa does not matter.

But the choice of rhetorical device is also of course non-arbitrary beyond poetry. To make sense of the quantum realm by means of conceptions belonging to the classical realm, analogy is sometimes the only option, as in explaining superposition of quantum states by the figure of a cat in a box which is simultaneously both dead and alive until an observation occurs. Here analogy is the choice for purposes of illustration. Sometimes it is not clear whether a description is intended literally or metaphorically: does the collapse of the wave function consist in a bifurcation of the universe's forward history, as in many-worlds theory, or choice of a unique forward history? There are those who take bifurcation literally, and those who say that although there are possible alternatives, the one and only real universe is whichever is realised by 'choice' of one the alternative futures. In the former case talk of bifurcating universes is literal, in the latter case talk of 'choice' of one possible future is metaphorical. There are reformulations of the latter view available that would obviate the need for metaphor.

It might be asked what importance attaches to getting a clear conception of the nature of metaphor. The answer has already been given in the opening paragraphs above, in regard to taking the metaphor of metaphor as illumination. There is much less risk of a simile or an analogy, when understood as such, being an *ignus fatuus* leading one astray. How metaphor is controlled in the process of theorising, how the disanalogies by definition present in the relationship between source and target are discounted and the interpretative power of the metaphorical illumination allowed to do its work, are questions for case by case uses of the device, most especially where there is no alternative means of expressing a conceptual insight. History presents us with familiar examples of metaphors taken as so close to

     The Metaphysics of Experience

being literal identifications that they seemed indeed literal: nature as clockwork, the nervous system as a telephone exchange, God as an astronaut, the brain as a computer. One can readily see how they can seem so given cases where the identification is indeed literal – 'the heart is a pump' – *looking* like metaphors without being so.

The same danger does not occur with the other two figures. To say *X is like Y* is not to mislead anyone into thinking that X is very close to being Y, or is *very* like Y in some ontologically suggestive way, still less *is* Y. The potential for slippage lies in the mimicking by the 'is' of metaphor of the 'is' of identity. This suggests a further thought, and perhaps a research project: that whereas the cognitive outcomes of uses of metaphors and similes is the same, the underlying mechanisms at work are different. The cognitive act involved in understanding *that* a metaphor has illuminated its target and *how* it has done so is something richer and deeper than, and different from, the cognitive act of comparison *simpliciter.* In this respect understanding metaphor is like understanding metonymy (the speech-act of using 'the White House' to mean the presidential component of US government, or 'the crown' to mean the monarchy). Arguably, metonymy is a form of metaphor, or at least exploits the same kind mechanism, this mechanism consisting in a transitive power of cross-applying conceptual content. In the case of metonymy this is used for the lesser (though hardly unimportant) task of fixing reference rather than illuminating some terrain of thought or theory, but with the same process of *semantic assignment by substitution* at work. As this indicates, the difference here is that there is much more to the uses of metaphor than the use of metonymy, and something cognitively different going on in both these cases from simile and analogy recognised as such.

This relates to the question of what it is one knows, or knows how to do, when one grasps a conceptual content, obviously a key factor in the cross-application of content for achieving metaphor's purposes. A simple case is given by a dog knowing that he is about to be taken for a walk; when he sees his master putting on his hat – this being the signal that a walk is in immediate prospect – he makes the association (draws the inference?) and thus illustrates how one thing 'means' another. This is what is at issue in the case of metonymy, and in part, but only in part, what is at issue in the case of metaphor.

This in turn suggests a distinction between complete and incomplete metaphor. The target in 'Napoleon is a whirlwind' is Napoleon's military career, of which a complete account can be given if someone asks for a justification for the metaphor's application; but the target in metaphors offered to make sense of quantum phenomena is something for which the metaphor is a rough guide merely, nothing more being sayable. In this kind of case the metaphor is *essentially* incomplete; it is this case that shows that the cross-application of conceptual content at work, here viewing the metaphor as a signal or cue that picks out and illuminates the target content, is only partial and *at best* only so. A taxonomy of metaphors would have its roots in this distinction, but it would not be a taxonomy of function, nor of effectiveness; it would mainly show which metaphors could be substituted by an analogy or even a simile, and which are irreducible.

These thoughts are schematic, but they suggest that there is a matrix of connections, in the cognitive architecture that instantiates concepts, around which resources of sense-making travel. There is no doubt that new knowledge offers new possibilities for illumination by metaphor, as history abundantly shows: the computer metaphor for the brain was not possible before the computer, and the productive power of metaphor is equally well illustrated by a metaphorical move in the opposite direction, yielding the idea of neural networks. One could proliferate examples. In cognitive psychology, in epistemology, and in the intrinsic interest of metaphor in literary and linguistic respects, there is much to explore. For the discussion so far the primary interest is the often irreducible role of metaphor in the resources of discourse-presupposing conceptual schemes.

But it also suggests an analogy of its own, or perhaps something more than an analogy if the idea can be made out, bearing on the question of the relation between reduced and reducing discourses. In an attempt to reductively assert a relation between phenomena referred to in different discourses, might it be fruitful to consider whether either stands to the other as in effect a metaphor for it (that the 'is' of identity is the 'is' of metaphor)? For example: the thought that the reduced discourse of mental phenomena might stand in such a relation to the reducing discourse of neurology would be suggestive in cashing out the ideas of correlation between mental contents and neural events or the 'supervenience' of the former on the latter when exceptionless covariance is predicated. If so, illumination substitutes for explanation, and thereby – to anticipate a further possibility – explains why deferral of metaphysical conclusions need make no difference to epistemology. Another and more immediately plausible way of adumbrating the point is to ask what is meant by saying e.g. that talk of pain is 'shorthand' for talk of C-fibre firing. The obvious response is to say that shorthand is a form of metonymy; but the achievement of metonymy is effected by metaphoric transfer of content from the reducing phenomenon by means of the metonymic expression (from the phenomenon of the presidential aspect of government of the United States to reference to 'the White House'). The claim would then be that *talk* of pain is 'metaphoric', or some analogy of being so, relative to *talk* of C-fibre activation (not – note! – that pain is 'unreal').

This, for the moment, is a gesture; but in regard to the proposals in the next two sections and particularly §7 *Enquiry and Modality* concerning the family of aspirations to *clarification, explication, understanding, modelling* and *explaining*, the role of metaphor and analogy does such heavy lifting that questions arise about their adequacy in all cases, suggesting that something more determinate is required to explain the success achieved in the processes of enquiry. There the focus is on the consideration that enquiry is as much if not more about *making sense* as about *finding out how things are*.

§6

Reduction and Communicability

In the discourse of perceptual experience sortal concepts of natural and artificial kinds, these latter referred to by general terms and (where these differ) collective terms, play a central role (Locke's 'the greatest part of words'), and reinforce the point insisted upon here that understanding the ontologies implicit in grammar ('grammatical ontology') of this discourse is to be assimilated to understanding grammatical ontology in general. That this seems unintuitive is the product of theories of natural kinds and reference to them, natural kinds being considered as groupings of the 'real things' in the empirically-encountered world argued to be the result of the way 'nature carves itself at its joints', a matter of great significance on this view because of the implications for science. But if the empirically-encountered world – the phenomenal world – is a virtual reality posited by creatures of human scale and cognitive endowments, articulated by an epistemically utilitarian and paraconsistent scheme for organising experience, then no kinds are natural in the standardly proposed sense; all kinds are 'artificial' in being the projected arrangements that suit those cognitive needs. If kinds are natural in the intended sense, it will be because their articulations are determined by how things are sorted in a reducing theory.

As this suggests, an immediate challenge to the view that kinds are ('merely') projected arrangements answering to cognitive needs in perceptual experience is the sortal realists' case for thinking its way about how things are in that experience, for it receives strong support from the sciences that straddle the classical horizon. Consider the most salient examples, viz. the biological sciences and biochemistry, geology, and applications of nuclear physics to energy-generation and immensely destructive weaponry. The evolution of taxonomic theory in biology post-Linnaeus is a ready instance of these examples, moving from (to put matters crudely) taxonomy based on outward appearance to genetics (in some earlier phases of the discussion, 'internal structure'), with implications for a revival of a doctrine of real essences.[1] The response to this from the viewpoint of the stand taken here is to parallel the observation made above about the 'brain-mind', itself a phenomenon to which neuropsychology boot-strappingly attributes phenomena-organising activity. But this does not exclude recognising that even on the assumption that perceptual experience ranges over a domain of virtual entities on the proximal side of the horizon, the resources for the explanatory models that successfully collect them into kinds are drawn from the extension of perception's capacities by means of instruments ranging from electron microscopes to particle colliders, generating and supporting powerful explanatory or at least applicable (via technology) theories about what lies on the distal side, inferred from the proximal phenomena (observables) and then in turn employed to see the phenomena in their light. The achievement of enquiry by these means is sometimes

---

[1]See S. Kripke, *Naming and Necessity* (Harvard University Press 1980); Grayling, 'Internal Structure and Essence' *Analysis* 42 (1982).

to draw some of what lies on the distal side into the proximal side – the straddling effect – but frequently if not indeed typically to justify treating the theory in question realistically.

In the practice of science the pragmatic motivation for doing so might either defer – in the sense of 'deferral' to be explicated here (§8) – or be regarded as settling the question of concern to the philosopher as to whether or not it is literally right to treat the theories realistically, at very least those in play in fundamental physics. But this philosophical concern is unavoidable if the assumption is made that the enquiries in question are *en route* to an account of ultimate reality; the metaphysical goal. On the argument here, if achievement of that goal is to be regarded as *essentially* deferrable then the pragmatic motivation of the scientist turns out to be not merely enough (and again, powerfully so) but right.

The theories in question are, in a general but literal sense, the product of inferences to the best explanation. One can note that a preliminary doubt about the literal realism option is raised by consideration of methodological principles governing enquiry: the drive to economy and simplicity in the laws. Viewing a theory as an explanatory model of the underlying mechanisms on the distal side invites questions about the relation of models constructed on such principles to the messy observables of which they are offered as an explanation, accordingly invoked as an account of their causal grounds. That relation shares features with the relation of a map to a terrain in being in part an idealisation that reduces the variety in the phenomena to generalisations (§7). At least two but at significant points related perspectives on this point invite consideration. One is the family of anti-realist views in the philosophy of science, the other is the question of reduction.

The outlines and principal points at issue in the realism-anti-realism debate in the philosophy of science are as familiar as the debate itself is extensive. I shall not reprise them but will pray in aid the claim that the thrust of scientific anti-realism is persuasively consistent, at very least, with the argument here, while scientific realism controverts it outright.[2] A formal defence of scientific anti-realism in these pages is in any case unnecessary because the considerations shortly to be adduced about kinds and reduction achieve the same end.

Before considering the question of reduction itself it is necessary to look first at the question of discourse about kinds because considerations about this bear directly on it. From the discussion of general terms earlier it is readily inferable what direction an account of sortals will take. And the entrance to this is in turn the question of how talk of kinds in the discourse of perceptual experience works.

A discussion of this latter matter could be short-circuited by invoking as established the claim, in the argument (in §2) that all reference goes via sense. A crucial point at issue in discussion of kinds is whether this is so, given argument to the claim that *natural* kind terms designate rigidly. On such a view, concepts of natural kinds are forced on perceivers by independent facts about kinds – independent, that is, of the perceptual endowments and activities of perceivers – because nature carves itself at its joints, and perceivers are obliged therefore to follow its articulations at risk of both theoretical and practical failure. This view predicates scientific realism. The opposed claim that the kinds into which nature is sorted in perceptual discourse are projections from the needs and convenience of creatures of human scale and endowments, *ipso facto* entails scientific anti-realism. Thus does the argument about sortals and the associated consequence for reduction arrive at the same conclusion as the latter.

---

[2]See for just two of many Nancy Cartwright, *How the Laws of Physics Lie* (Oxford University Press 1983); Darrell P. Rowbottom, 'The Instrumentalist's New Clothes', *Philosophy of Science* 78(5) (2011): 1200–1211. See also van Fraasen and Fine notes 3 and 4 in §1.

Begin by assembling some reminders. An illustrative one is the 'Twin Earth' discussion. My twin and I drink, bathe in and talk about phenomenologically-indistinguishable stuff we both call 'water', but by hypothesis the chemical make-up of the substances are different.[3] The aim of the thought-experiment's original proposal by Putnam was to demonstrate that two platitudes about meaning are inconsistent; one, that meaning determines extension, the other, that meaning is determined by the content of speakers' mental states. The first platitude implies that the meaning of 'water' in my twin's mouth is different from its meaning in mine, the second implies that it is the same.[4]

In the debate pursuant to Putnam's proposal various moves were offered to resolve the inconsistency. One is to enrich the first platitude by relativizing it in a suitable way to context. Another was to distinguish between broad and narrow meaning, broad meaning determining extension and narrow meaning consisting in what governs a speaker's use of 'water' by being psychologically manifest to him in his grasp of it. But both the thought-experiment and these responses are based on assuming certain theses about natural kinds, unexamined in the debate itself, which load the dice against the second platitude from the off. Also unexamined is the misleading assumption that it is intelligible in the first place to regard the 'content of a speaker's mental states' individualistically even apart from considerations about broad meaning.

The first of these assumptions is that natural kind terms designate rigidly *in virtue* of the fact that nature carves itself at its joints, a

---

[3]The discussion here draws on Grayling, 'Concept-Reference and Natural Kinds.' In *Truth, Meaning and Realism* (Continuum 2007). References to the relevant texts in Putnam, Kripke, Frege and Wiggins occur in this source and are in the offing throughout.

[4]The two assumptions that my twin and I are atom-for-atom identical and that psychological states are determined by neurological states are taken for granted.

conception entailing that the real natures (in effect, essences) of kinds can and often do transcend perceivers' recognitional capacities (and correlatively that it is of at least some of these that science, realistically conceived, is seeking to identify, by achieving more penetrative recognitional capacities via theories about what is on the distal side). The idea that the individuating essence of a kind consists in its 'internal structure' or, differently its origin (for example its genetic make-up, as e.g. in differentiating Bengal tigers from Tasmanian tigers) are open to challenge by arguments that destabilise the idea of 'natural kinds' itself even on realistic grounds.[5]

The second of these assumptions ignores an essential constraint on 'knowing the meaning of a term', which is that what is thus grasped has to be so far conformable to what others in the linguistic community grasp that communication between them is possible. Grant that associations attached to a term in the idiolects of speakers might be individual to them and even eccentric, it remains that they cannot be communicating with each other unless there is a significant common ground of understanding. This point is important for all its obviousness – an obviousness overlooked in the debate – because what Putnam described as 'stereotypes' and Wiggins as 'conceptions' (in his account, a conception is 'a way of grasping a concept'), these being what speakers grasp securely enough to achieve reference to a kind whose nature nevertheless transcends their finite epistemic capacities, proceed by borrowing enough from a description theory of reference to make communication possible while preserving

---

[5]In the offing, Quine on essence and *de re* modality, see e.g. 'Reference and Modality' and 'Three Grades of Modal Involvement' respectively in *From a Logical Point of View*, 2nd ed. (Harper and Row 1961) and *The Ways of Paradox* (Harvard University Press 1976). For arguments variously on internal structure and origin, Grayling *ibid* and 'Internal Structure and Essence' *Analysis* 42 (1982); W. A. Collins, 'Types, Rigidity and a Posteriori Necessity' *Midwest Studies* XII (1988); Tim Crane, 'All the Difference in the World' *Philosophical Quarterly* 41 (1991).

realism about kinds.[6] But the very fact that this compromise has to be made signals the implausibility of any view parasitic on the Fregean idea that senses are fully objective courtesy of the independently real nature of the referents that the senses present even when detecting the referents falls short of the receptive competence of a speaker to do so. This iterates the complaint that an anti-realist about senses makes in saying that to grasp a sense (to 'know the meaning') must be a function not just of a speaker's epistemic capacities but what he understands about his sharing them with other speakers. To put the point another way: under a communicability constraint, to know the meaning of a term is also and essentially to know what core meaning, at least, it has in the linguistic community.

It might appear that there need be no inconsistency in granting both points on the grounds that speakers can share a common-enough understanding of a sortal to enable communication while it is nevertheless the case that some or all of the content of what they grasp lies beyond their recognitional capacities. This just seems obvious when one views it from the point of view of 'discovering more about a kind' in the course of enquiry, for what is discovered was previously not part of the grasped content; it lay beyond it until that point. But this predicates a jump from incomplete and extendable content to objective and determinate content, and it is this that is questionable. To infer from the fact that enquiry can add content to a concept to the view that there is determinate content that could even in principle lie beyond speakers' recognitional capacities is to commit to a fully Fregean view of objectivity. This distinguishes sortals from general terms such as 'red' with *intrinsically* vague borders of application, and requires that what makes the latter learnable and communicable is different from how *natural* kind sortals are

---

[6]References in Grayling, 'Concept Reference' in *Truth, Meaning and Realism* 2007.

learned and understood. Whereas artificial kind sortals are generally determinate in application by stipulation, to import a stipulative element into natural kind sortal definitions – by means of stereotypes or conceptions – is to create a hybrid unsustained even on empirical grounds: Linnaean criteria of classification by genus and species do not group birds and crocodilians together, whereas in modern zoological taxonomy they are related as the only current survivors of the clade *Archosauria*. On the stereotype-conception view, to learn how to use 'bird' and 'crocodile' in order to communicate successfully is to acquire grasp of nominal essences which are or can be wholly disjoint from their putative real essences. They act merely as a clue, as it were, or prompt for what can nevertheless turn out to have incorrect implications – not just in the sense that our understanding of them can be adjusted and extended by new discoveries, but that we are wholly wrong about them. It is fun to learn that (on current and well-motivated taxonomies) blackberries are not berries and that tomatoes are berries, but the entailment from this to the claim that what we learn when we learn the use of these terms is only partly or even not at all what they 'actually' mean is enough of a surprise to require an explanation.

One of the chief motivations for Frege's view was the desire to secure a guarantee of public meaning. That might seem to be the same goal as the communicability constraint aims at, but at the over-reaching price of accepting that the fact that the meaning of a term can transcend what an individual speaker subjectively associates with the term applies to the linguistic community collectively; that, in short, the meaning of the term can be unknowable. Such a view might be able to accommodate the fact that the meanings of terms undergo change in a language's history (for example by saying that speakers' knowledge increasingly approximates to the term's 'real' meaning) but it falls foul of learnability constraints. These turn on use and speakers' intentions – Gricean constraints[7] – and they are ineliminable in explaining meaning, a point captured by noting how it would be to hold simultaneously that dictionaries define a given term's meaning by reporting speakers' usages and yet that it does not mean what they use it to mean. What seems to be going wrong here is that a fallacy of composition has been committed. The meaning of a term is not what any individual speaker chooses, like Humpty Dumpty, to attach to it, but that does not entail that it is independent of what is meant by it in the linguistic community.[8] The fault lies in the move from 'independent of any individual speaker' to 'independent of the linguistic community as a whole'. Indeed, the fact that publicity of meaning can be secured by intersubjectively constrained conformities of use makes Fregean objectivity of sense, even if it were plausible, unnecessary.

This point accommodates anti-individualistic accounts of meaning in general, because their correct insistence that meaning has broad content is readily made out by noting that what successful communication between speakers triangulates upon is the ontology of the conceptual scheme they share. As Burge notes, 'the meanings of many terms – and the identities of many concepts – are what they are even though what the individual knows about the meaning or concept may be insufficient to determine it uniquely'.[9] This suggests a correction to Putnam's 'meanings just ain't in the head' to 'meanings

---

[7]See e.g. Paul Grice, 'Utterer's Meaning and Intentions' *The Philosophical Review* 78 (1969); objections to Grice's approach e.g. Mark Platts, *Ways of Meaning*, 2nd edn. (MIT Press 1997) include saying that it cannot accommodate the meaning of unuttered sentences; a Gricean reply might conjoin considerations of compositionality and counterfactual circumstances of utterance.

[8]Grayling, 'Publicity, Stability, and "Knowing the Meaning"' in *Truth, Meaning and Realism* 2007.

[9]Tyler Burge, 'Philosophy of Language and Mind' *Philosophical Review* 101 (1992).

are partly in speakers' heads and wholly in our collective heads'. The case for saying so is as follows.

To grant, as we must, that language is essentially public, is to commit to recognising the implications of the fact that meanings must be learned in a public setting, and that criteria for correct use of expressions consists in the reciprocal government exercised by speakers over each others' linguistic performance. In part this aligns with Wittgenstein's strictures on private language and rule-following, though it diverges in requiring of speakers that they understand what it is to follow usage rules – hence the ineliminability of the narrow end of content. Accordingly it is not facts about an *objectively* conceived domain over which the discourse ranges that is required for conformity with the rules; indeed this is not even a necessary let alone sufficient condition for doing so, as demonstrated by the cases where the domains are fictional or abstract. Conjoin this thought with the claim that understanding the discourse of perceptual experience (and by extension scientific enquiry) is to be assimilated to discourses about such domains, and we see that *intersubjectively* constituted domains are sufficient to provide the basis for conformity. What makes this more than a commonplace, as it is for some views, is that it exposes the persistent tendency to think, or desire, that there has to be something left over, namely, how things really are independently of how we think and talk; that even if the phenomena are all there are in some cases, in others – and in the perceptual and scientific cases particularly – there has to be a noumenon that partly or wholly escapes, and may forever escape, our capacity to know it. That there is something right about thinking this is what considerations about the strategic role of realist assumptions in enquiry and the notion of deferral will be invoked to explain (§§7,8); what is questionable about it is how it makes aspects of knowing and learning meaning unintelligible when the putative referents of terms lie inaccessibly, and even in principle so, in the noumenon.

In §1 it was noted that the hold that some form of realism derived from the intuitions of naïve realism has on our conceptual imaginations is extremely powerful, to the extent that it renders unattractive the idea that a domain is 'merely' intersubjectively constituted. This is to fail to see that such a domain can be as robust, causative and resistant as anyone wants from '*real* reality', and that some important domains are. This point is made out more fully in §8. For present purposes matters can be put as a question: on what grounds does one say that extending, refining, developing a concept consists in discovering more about an independently pre-existing state of things of which the earlier history of the concept gave only a partial grasp? The answer lies in both the utility of doing so and the experience of doing so; we frame the process of enquiry not as creation but as discovery because developments of concepts can bring unexpected novelties into view. For an anti-realist about mathematics this might be explained by claiming that not all of the implications of a given mathematical structure are apparent until other elements of it are in place. The point generalises. But how does this entail commitment to the idea that *there are* wholly and even in principle inaccessible recognition-transcendent facts beyond the limits of our concepts? To say so resembles claiming that a boundary can be drawn not because we postulate a distal side for doing so as a matter of theoretical or practical utility but because there actually is one even though we have not yet got, or even can never get, access to it. The practice of pushing conceptual boundaries further out underwrites this latter idea, and fully explains the conceptual convenience of assuming it as an essential feature of enquiry, but it does not entail it. Here another set of considerations requires discussion, regarding the role of imaginability, conceivability and modality in enquiry and the formation of conceptual schemes: see §7.

The net effect of the foregoing is to assimilate the learning and use of expressions in perceptual and scientific discourses to discourses generally. This is just the point at issue in the overall argument; in this particular connection the conclusion it invites is that natural kind terms are general terms, not a special subset of them individuated by an irreducible commitment to realism about their domain. This conclusion cashes out in identifying the practice of learning more about a subject matter as consisting in bringing more into a general term's extension, or finding good motivations for adjusting its criteria of application, or replacing it with a better (more adequate or effective) classificatory convention outright – of which the standout form is eliminative reduction. That provides an umbrella description of what enquiry in fact consists in.

By 'reduction' I mean theoretical not entity reduction; the latter might better be characterised as analysis, in at least one of its forms.[10] The chief aim of effecting a reduction is to explain a given subject matter by revealing what the items addressed by it are and why they are that way, all the better if it provides, in relevant contexts, a handle for manipulation or control. A theoretical reduction might and often does involve analysis of the items in question, but equally often the items are themselves the referents of terms whose sense is determined by the theory, so that the reduction of one theory to another is achieved by analysis of the items referred to in the reduced

---

[10]There is a discussion to be had about the family of concepts consisting of reduction, definition, and the several kinds of analysis distinguished by e.g. Russell and Moore, and their relation to such philosophical tasks as explicating, clarifying and 'making sense', failure to attend to which results in the potential confusions that arise in claiming of some concept, for a notable example that of 'truth', that it is indefinable. See Grayling on Davidson, 'Truth and Indefinability' in *Truth, Meaning and Realism*, 39–54 and *passim*.

theory into items referred to in the reducing theory, or to elimination of them outright.

Two familiar and major reductive enterprises occur in the philosophy of mind and in the project of unifying the sciences. The former is a chapter of the latter in that reduction of psychological contents to neurological events which in turn, via biochemistry itself in turn reducible to physics, places mental phenomena in a complete description of the universe as a realm of physical laws, in the idealised state the laws being as few and simple as possible. The question whether this ambition is to be understood as the actual and potentially realisable target of the enterprise or as an organising principle of enquiry makes no practical difference, but an enormous philosophical difference.

Distinctions are sometimes drawn between reduction by translation of the terms of one discourse or theory into the terms of another, respectively the reduced and reducing discourses, and derivation of the phenomena of the reduced discourse from those of the reducing discourse. Granting a difference between translation and derivation, both procedures ultimately aim at providing an explanation or at least illumination of the phenomena in the reduced discourse, for translation – although it might have clarification or increased facility with the data as its immediate terminus – is propaedeutical to derivation. In the Positivist case for translation into a 'common language' for science the project aims to achieve an eventual unification of science via shriving it of any subjectivity; the language is to contain nothing that turns on the individual intensional associations or perspectives of scientists.[11]

---

[11]See e.g. Rudolf Carnap, 'On the Character of Philosophic Problems' trans. W. M. Malisoff (Carnap Project: Benson No. 1934-1); Otto Neurath, 'Radical Physicalism and the "Real World"' in *Philosophical Papers 1913–1946*, ed. R. S. Cohen and M. Neurath (Reidel 1983); Nancy Cartwright, *The Dappled World: A Study of the Boundaries of Science* (Cambridge University Press 1999).

Taking translation to be a step towards derivation involves understanding the relation between the terms in which each discourse is couched. In Hempel's view there is no requirement that the definitions of reduced by reducing terms should be analytic, it is enough that they should have the same extension. But even this imposes a constraint that, on eliminativist views particularly, is dispensable; in what Nagel calls 'heterogeneous reduction', terms in the reduced discourse might have no extensional equivalence to terms in the reducing discourse, the phenomena they denote being indirectly derived via bridging laws, or disappearing altogether as in the case of mental states under a physicalist reduction predicating the identity of such states with states of the nervous system.[12]

As this last point shows, a key question is whether the phenomena in the reduced and reducing discourses are causally related or identical, or in cases where the terms of the reduced discourse are chimerical (as argued by Patricia Churchland) vanish altogether and are replaced by those of a different discourse which therefore bears no relation to them.[13] Do phenomena referred to in the reducing discourse cause phenomena referred to in the reduced discourse, or are they the same thing under different descriptions? On this latter view, as in the chimerical view, the desideratum of ontological simplification is achieved.[14] But an interesting divergence of opinion follows; whereas elimination is a strong motivation in the philosophy of mind, in physics derivation is arguably enough; statements about the relation between phenomena in two discourses one of which is

---

[12]Carl Hempel, *Aspects of Scientific Explanation* (Free Press 1965); Ernst Nagel, *The Structure of Science* (Routledge 1961).

[13]Patricia Churchland, *Neurophilosophy: Toward a Unified Science of the Mind-Brain* (MIT 1986).

[14]Jaegwon Kim, *Explanatory Realism, Causal Realism, and Explanatory Exclusion* (Midwest Studies 12) (Elsevier 1988); Churchland, *Neurophilosophy*.

physicalistic need only take conditional form, and do not have to be biconditionals still less assertions of identity.

An apparent problem with derivation is how it accounts for the fact that reduced discourses come often enough to be seen as containing falsehoods and require (if they are not eliminated) adjustment accordingly. Reduction is in this way revisionary.[15] Where the reduced discourse survives it accordingly does so in an altered state. A major virtue of this outcome short of complete explanation of the phenomena is the achievement of better organisation of the reduced discourse itself.

Another and this time not merely apparent problem is the relation of observation to the theories articulated in both the reduced and reducing discourses. Given the undeniable fact that one does not simply see but always sees-as, and that seeing-as is conditioned by the theory, implicit or otherwise, governing the act, an account is required of how observation confirms or infirms theory.[16] In its simplest form the question is troubling enough, but it gives added weight to the problem of multiple realisability.[17] This not only disrupts the ambition to find identities between phenomena referred to in the reduced and reducing discourses but even the project of stating bridge laws that relate them. In the case of physicalism about mind, a resort is to treat correlation (or 'supervenience' when exceptionless covariance is predicated) as carrying the load; the physical correlates of mental phenomena are what are taken to be observed in fMRI investigations, and implicitly treated as doing as much as is attainable in the way of explanation of them.

---

[15]K. F. Schaffner, 'Approaches to Reduction' *Philosophy of Science* 34 (1967).

[16]One can go all the way back to Neurath to see that the problem infects the very roots of explanation.

[17]In the offing, Jerry Fodor, 'Special Sciences, or the Disunity of Science' *Synthese* 28 (1974); Hilary Putnam, *Mind, Language and Reality* (Cambridge University Press 1975).

Two responses to the multiple realisability problem offered to dispose of it are either to say that it is a problem only for identity theories and their weaker analogue of biconditional bridge laws, or to say that a reducing discourse entails a revision of the reduced discourse in light of it; the reducing discourse settles what form the reduced discourse is to take, if it survives as a discourse at all.[18]

Reductionisms are familiarly taxonomised into ontological, epistemic and methodological forms. I suggested above that reduction of entities might better be understood in terms of analysis, one typical form being analysis into constituents. A biological organism analysed into cells and molecules might be hoped to provide via an account of their functions an account of the nature and behaviour of the organism itself. This plays a part in both ontological and methodological reduction. Ontological reduction is 'ontological' because it turns on an antecedent metaphysical commitment; it views the entities of the structure and the whole physicalistically. Methodological reduction treats the analysis of entities into constituents as yielding the required causal explanation of the organism's nature and behaviour. The conjunction of the two appears to yield epistemic reduction, in which a reduced theory is explained by – is deducible from – the reducing theory, as for example in biological discourse's reduction to biochemistry. But 'appears' is the *mot juste*, because of a multiple realisability problem – more accurately, both one-many and many-one realisations – in the relations between constituents and higher level structures. This is especially notable in biology. In any case, methodological reduction can provide explanations independently of whether total reduced theory has been underwritten by total reducing theory, as Waters argued; this blocks treating methodological

---

[18]C. A. Hooker, *Toward a General Theory of Reduction* (Dialogue 20) (Cambridge University Press 1981).

reduction as merely a component of epistemic reduction, in that such reductions can be explanatory or at very least useful in organising the phenomena referred to in the reduced discourse and sometimes manipulating them, without requiring that the total theory of the reduced discourse be deducible from the total theory of the reducing discourse.

Everything so far said presupposes that the phenomena referred to in both reduced and reducing discourses can be represented in ways that are sufficiently determinate to leave no doubt as to whether the required relationship has been established between them. In its most acute form the problem is apparent in the relationship between a model and what it models, between an idealisation as expressed by an equation and the messy phenomena of nature.[19] In these and allied cases a suggestive move is to look for resources in analogy, metonymy and metaphor to unpack the idea of representation, taking as a base case the way a symbol – that of the international Red Cross organisation is a paradigm instance – achieves what is meant by representing and 'standing for'. Obviously, the way models, equations and whole theories relate to their target phenomena is not *merely* symbolic in at least most cases, and in numerous cases of reduction the effect is genuinely explanatory or at least such that the phenomena referred to in the reduced discourse are rendered intelligible, often in ways that admit of successful manipulation and control of them. But to explain the various relations of reduction at work is to explain their 'more than merely symbolic' nature in this sense.

These observations merely skim the surface of what, underneath – and not least in the philosophy of biology which is paradigmatically a family of sciences straddling the classical horizon – is a tangled set of

---

[19]See Cartwright, *The Dappled World*; A. Potochnik, *Idealization and the Aims of Science* (University of Chicago Press 2017).

problems in making out an account of reduction that accommodates its species and purposes, individuable by theoretical context. As this point suggests, the temptation to provide a unitary account of procedures by which a reduced discourse relates to its reducing discourse is at least suspect for the reasons given. But for the purposes here there are several points that merit salience, and which align with the points to be made in the next section about enquiry.

The first thing to note is that the concept of 'reduction' itself is a metaphor, and an irreducible one. This remains so across the more circumstantial renditions of the methods and aims offered by way of talk of translation, derivation and explanation. The second is to note that even a survey of this generality shows that incomplete reduction, that is, reduction which does not achieve or even aspire to achieve elimination of the referents of terms in the reduced discourse via identity or chimera claims (and in the latter case of the discourse itself), 'works' in providing explanations or at least useful organisation and sometimes control of the phenomena referred to in the reduced discourse. Incomplete reduction might entail acceptance of the concept of emergent properties; it might require beginning from holistic conceptions of the target phenomena to enable selection of a direction of enquiry into what will yield an account of them that is explanatory or at least illuminating, and this in turn might necessitate invoking teleological considerations. And it might well, via 'as if' moves, itself turn on ineliminable deployment of analogy or metaphor. Whether complete or incomplete, reduction requires distinguishing what is to count as 'internal' from what is 'external' in the phenomena (in the case of causal explanations, identifying which is the cause and which the effect), as well as distinguishing the phenomena themselves from their environments.

Reduction has at least the aim of making the aspect of the world it addresses more intelligible to us; it also has the pragmatic aim in relevant cases of increasing our ability to manipulate and control that aspect of the world to our benefit; it has some of its principal roots in the project of unifying the sciences; and beyond these it has the implicit metaphysical aim of revealing the nature of ultimate reality. At its most modest, a reductive enterprise is well seen as strategic in nature, as a regulative ideal whose government of enquiry is normative, justified by its intelligibility and pragmatic yields.[20] Viewed in this way, reductive enterprises, in all but the last aspiration mentioned – the metaphysical one – are wholly epistemic. This requires discussion of certain highly relevant considerations about processes, and constraints upon them, of enquiry.

---

[20]K. F. Schaffner, *Discovery and Explanation in Biology and Medicine* (Chicago University Press 1993).

§7

Enquiry and Modality

One major strand in epistemology has traditionally concerned itself with refuting sceptical challenges to knowledge claims within particular domains, in particular the perceptual domain. This approach often appeals to considerations such as perceptual relativities (bent sticks in water, objects looking small from far away and large close up), subjective factors (secondary qualities, indexicality, hallucination), and the prevalent risk of error as a datum both in perception and reasoning. Scepticism in this form is *problematic* scepticism, threatening agniology for the domain, or at least reducing the prospects for enquiry to defeasible belief at best, asserting in sum that the best evidence for p is always consistent with the falsity of p.

That this was a central problematic for epistemology is demonstrated by discussion of the question from *Theaetetus* through to Sextus Empiricus to Descartes to forms of idealism both transcendental and absolute, and on to phenomenalism in Anglophone philosophy in the twentieth century. In each case, apart from the Academic appeal to 'suspension of judgment', these discussions prompted accounts of what can nevertheless be known, and how. Some of these accounts proceed by accepting agniology for the challenged domain (standardly in these debates, the perceptual domain; the appearances) and offering an account of what there really is behind it or differently from it, as in Plato and idealism. Some respond by offering refutation of the sceptical arguments themselves; for example, phenomenalism seeks to show that encounter with entities and events in the empirical domain consists in constructions out of actual and possible sense experience and are (putatively) verifiable by reference to them, while others seek to show that the sceptical considerations themselves are ill-formed (for example Ryle's polar concept argument; Austen's attention to subtleties of meaning).[1]

In the case of responses to sceptical challenges that seek to show that knowledge is possible, scepticism is treated as *methodological* rather than problematic, that is, as a route to the establishment of knowledge claims in the domain. Descartes employed the sceptical considerations he adduces in the first *Meditation* – the *malin genie* thought experiment providing the most inclusive sceptical challenge to all possible knowledge claims – in this way. The strategy treats sceptical considerations as identifying the challenges that have to be met by enquiry; generalising the technique provides an interesting purchase on the nature of enquiry itself. The following is a survey of principal such challenges.

In the domain of perceptual experience, and by extension via instruments and the medium of applicable theory to empirical experience, the first challenge is presented by the fact of the scale at which enquiry begins, together with the finite nature of the enquirers' cognitive endowments even as potentiated by instrumental means. For human enquirers this places them at a severely restricted starting point relative to the domain within which its initially accessible region is taken to lie. The metaphor of a 'pinhole' is apt here; it is as if we

---

[1] The extent of this survey renders providing references for all of it impracticable; I take it that a reader of this text will know them or know how to find them. In *The Refutation of Scepticism* and *Scepticism and the Possibility of Knowledge* I adapted a Kantian approach which will be recognised as ancestral to the arguments here.

see everything beyond the perceptually accessible through a pinhole. The reachable regions – those accessed instrumentally and by means of theory – constitute the empirical domain. Inference to the nature and causal operations of what lies on the distal side of the pinhole is constrained by what sense can be made of it by the means available on the proximal side, including, in the case of fundamental physics, mathematics. By now familiarly, much of that sense-making in this latter domain can be effected *only* mathematically, and otherwise relies on metaphor and analogy to provide an at best approximate grasp. A question arises as to the extent to which the use of metaphor and analogy is irreducible in a sense-making enterprise where this fact is inescapable or perhaps not even recognised – unlike their use to illustrate quantum phenomena, which is strictly heuristic – and what this entails regarding what can be claimed as known in such cases.

A second, allied, consideration is the question of the relation between models and maps of a subject area and the subject area itself. By their nature models and maps impose a neatness on their target subjects by exclusion of details and exceptions, with the aim of comprehensibly though not comprehensively organising the phenomena addressed. In doing so by way of acknowledged idealisation or approximation they can prompt such claims as Cartwright makes to the effect that 'the laws of physics lie'.[2]

Two further considerations allied to this concern the limitations colloquially labelled the 'Hammer Problem' and the 'Lamplight Problem' – the first is summed up in the saying that if your instrument is a hammer everything looks like a nail; the second in the observation that you only see where you look, and indeed can only look where you have a chance of seeing (the label invokes the scenario

---

[2]See note 16 in §3.

of looking for lost keys under a street light at night). The analogies are illuminating. In the case of fundamental science, Wigner's question about the 'unreasonable effectiveness' of mathematics is a reminder of the hammer consideration, and a debate turns upon it.[3]

A fifth consideration is in turn allied to the two preceding. An umbrella term for it is the 'observer effect', and relates to possible interference with the subject of study made by the activity of investigating it. In the case of studies in, say, animal ethology the difficulty of obviating the effect is greater than in the case of, say, discounting the effect of staining in microscopy, the comparison illustrating the care required for controlling the kind and degree of interference. In quantum theory an experimental set-up is part of the system being experimented upon, and requires to be factored in; the idea that observation collapses the wave function plays a central role in Copenhagen interpretations of the theory, responses to which include the suggestion that the system itself, and perhaps the entire universe, acts as observer.[4]

An arguably more serious version of the observer effect is the propensity to 'read-in' from the assumptions and expectations of the theoriser, a problem particularly acute in history and the social sciences. But it is a risk not absent from enquiry in the natural sciences, where the expectations and theoretical commitments of enquirers can go so far as to determine what to count as relevant and irrelevant in the data, or to so shape the design of experiments and experimental equipment as to harvest only data selected in advance as the target of investigation, at risk of missing something.

---

[3]E. Wigner, 'The Unreasonable Effectiveness of Mathematics in the Natural Sciences' *Communications on Pure and Applied Mathematics* 13(1) (1960). See A. C. Grayling, *The Frontiers of Knowledge* (Viking 2021) 120–28.

[4]The idea that the entire system, indeed the entire universe as the system, acts as the observer, is promoted by observations of entanglement.

A seventh consideration is whether reduction of one domain to another (for example mental phenomena to neural events) is conceptually safe, in correctly identifying the correlates in the reduced and reducing discourses, in satisfying the aims of reduction in cases where it is incomplete, in accounting for emergent properties if the latter leaves danglers – in general in not introducing distortions or falsifications.

An eighth problem consists in inferring that a theory is true because it works. On the Pragmatists' theory of truth this would not be a problem, but there are many domains in which falsehoods are effective (politics is one) and truths obstructive (for example, to whatever consists in or follows from a desire that they be false). The Ptolemaic universe worked for predicting solar and lunar eclipses and planetary positions, and found a convincing way to explain the variability in planetary properties such as luminosity and size by employing the Hipparchian concept of epicycles. The model survived until acceptance of the Copernican view and its confirmation by telescopy one and a half millennia later; thereby serving as a cautionary tale in this regard.[5] It is a striking thought also that the powerful and successful theories both of the microstructure of matter and of cosmology are derived from the understanding so far gained of less than 5 per cent of what constitutes the mass density of the universe, 'dark matter' and 'dark energy' – so far inaccessible to investigation and presumed to exist by indirect observation only – constituting the rest.

---

[5]Newtonian theories of mechanics and gravitation are accurate to one part in a million, and predicate a view that is effective for scales greater than the very small and less than the very large, but fails in all fundamentals relating to space, time, radiation, and the constitution of matter and the forces operative upon it (electromagnetic, strong and weak nuclear) as described in the Standard Model of the atom.

There are psychological considerations in enquiry also, a chief one being what might be described as a 'closure problem', that is, the desire to have a finished view to hand that satisfies the natural need for explanatory completeness. This is a feature of what Kahneman identified as 'fast thinking' in the general populace: leaping to conclusions, accepting a view on inadequate grounds because it accords with what one wishes to believe.[6] In this sense it is a close cousin of reading-in. Although a common feature of popular attitudes, the risk it poses to more serious forms of enquiry is not null, though likely to be more prevalent in social than natural science.

A final consideration relates to the criteria employed when a choice of competing views cannot be adjudicated on grounds either internal to them or in a comparison of their efficacy in organising, predicting, and where relevant controlling the phenomena addressed. In such cases notions of simplicity, best conformity with neighbouring theory, even beauty, might be invoked, and when they are a question must arise as to their reliability. Invoking extra-theoretical criteria is not arbitrary, indeed can be well-motivated; relative simplicity is a desideratum for practical reasons. But evidently a risk attaches to treating their application as conclusive.

This survey is cursory, but it illustrates the kinds of thing that responsible enquiry has to take into account. If nothing else it indicates the precarities of enquiry; and challenges to meet the precarities can be formidable. With cognizance of them in the background, the next question is what the aims of enquiry are.

An obvious reply is: the achievement of knowledge. But what is meant by 'knowledge' takes a number of forms. One, and the chief desideratum, is determination of how things are in a domain which constitutes an explanatory account (what, why and how); as we say,

---

[6]D. Kahneman, *Thinking Fast and Slow* (Viking 2011).

getting to the truth about it. In light of the remarks about the concept of truth earlier, this translates into drawing the best supported and most effective picture of the domain, such that what is asserted of it has the properties of being reliable in inference, consistent with other propositions we likewise value, usable in evaluating other propositions, epistemically authoritative for the domain, normative for rationality, and more effective than competitors to it in organising the domain's subject-matter by the epistemic standards applied in the evaluation, thereby inviting agreement.

But 'knowledge' also consists in – at the same time or alternatively – the more diffuse but no less valuable enterprises of illuminating, providing a handle on, clarifying, organising, interpreting, simplifying, illustrating, delineating – in general 'making sense' of – the domain and what it contains. The list is redundant, but this last idea, 'making sense', captures the aim of enquiry in all its reach from attainment of knowledge that fully explains to attainment of these more diffuse results short of it. In light of the following remarks, the idea of making sense introduces a problem of its own, discussed below.

The notion of epistemic standards relates to what can be given the umbrella term of 'canons of enquiry' appropriate to a domain – an umbrella term because although all enquiry in general has to be responsible in the sense of fulfilling overarching obligations to be honest, careful, thorough, transparent, ethical and unbiased, these are themselves generalities that cash out in different ways according to the domain in question. A typical research protocol for the natural and quantitative social sciences at the minimum consists in specification of the objectives of the enquiry, its rationale, feasibility, design and methodology, the statistical or analytical evaluation of the data harvested, and plans for publication of the results. In presenting a proposal for research, information about the participants and their qualifications is standardly required, and (as is often the case) where funding is sought a timeline specified. For studies which raise ethical considerations, the consent of subjects, questions about confidentiality and privacy (including how data is stored) and conflicts of interest are on the agenda. Clarity on the balance of risks and benefits is essential in all cases. Submitting a proposal to review, and having its results examined and questioned by others with expertise in the field, are the bookends of a process that seeks to be accounted scrupulous.

Obviously enough, a research proposal (say, a PhD proposal) in literature – a study of the poetry of Keats, for example – dispenses with most of these requirements, but a convincing statement of the rationale, design and objectives remain a minimum. To think that talents for close reading and sensitivity to nuance are peculiar to literary or philosophical studies would be to ignore, in the natural and social sciences, the value of ingenuity in experimental design and the creativity involved in identifying a question to be answered. It might more often be the case that problem situations in the organised sciences offer themselves – one piece of research prompting the need for further research into a question raised by it – but the intellectual qualities of researchers themselves is often a key to innovative work. There are many impressive examples. From remarking that at the summer solstice the town of Syene in southern Egypt threw no shadows at midday whereas at Alexandria midday shadows were observable, Eratosthenes was able to determine the circumference of the earth (correctly to within 10 per cent). Robert Millikan's measurement of the charge on an electron (the oil drop experiment) is as clever in conception as it is simple, and required remarkable precision in being carried out. The work on neurogenesis by Jonas Frisen and colleagues at Sweden's Karolinska Institute is a paradigm of ingenuity: using the fact that atmospheric nuclear testing was banned after 1963 and that levels of radioactive carbon in DNA is measurable, the birth date of cells can be determined by the amount of C14 found in them; more before 1963, less afterwards. If the idea is ingenuous, the experimental design and procedure was equally so; isolating cell nuclei, purifiying the DNA contained in them, converting the carbon to graphite and subjecting it to mass spectrometry (having with great difficulty accumulated enough graphite from the cell source for spectrometry to be effective), required exceedingly painstaking work.

Science offers what is arguably the most disciplined and successful epistemology achieved by human beings, and it is no surprise therefore that social science makes efforts to bring the less tractable (because less public and repeatable, more variable and vague) phenomena of human subjectivity into the purview of quantitative methodologies. One or another social science enquiry might rely on data accumulated from questionnaires, hence on the barely controllable material of subjectivity, but the analysis of it relies on statistical techniques. Asking the right questions in the right way, and seeking to maximise objective elements in the answer (for example, on subjects' self-perceived levels of wellbeing it might be relevant to ask how often they have attended a doctor's surgery in the preceding year, for what reasons, and what treatment they received) is key. The benefits of statistical analyses across broad swathes of concern from epidemiology to public policy formulation, is undeniable. But so is the fact that aggregates, means, averages and norms are meshes of wide articulation through which much that is individual slips. The pixels of individual experience, invisible in the overall image, are explored in, for example, the very different enterprise of literature; distinctions within generalising concepts of significance to humanity in ethics, politics and elsewhere are achievable by philosophical scrutiny; in sum: the slogan is 'horses for courses'.

It is these thoughts that suggest a generic notion of canons of enquiry for a domain and its subdomains, specific for each. With respect to almost any claim the questions, 'How do you know?' or

'Why do you think that?' are relevant, and invite, indeed expect, an answer couched in terms of the relevant canon of enquiry.

These thoughts also recall the first challenge mentioned above, the 'pinhole problem' of the scale at which enquiry begins together with the finite nature of enquirers' cognitive endowments even as potentiated by instrumental means. It was remarked that this places enquirers at a restricted starting point. Two connected difficulties are exposed by this.

The first is that even at the proximal side of the pinhole, enquiry is as subject to the challenges listed above as enquiry into what lies on the distal side. Meeting the challenges is constrained by the limits on enquirers' endowments, however much extended by ingenuity in the design, methods and equipment deployed. We see through the window of human cognitive capacity, which means, in short, that we learn only what we are capable of learning. Successive steps in enquiry increase that capability by providing more means to learn, but at any point there is essential reference to the point from which the next step departs.

This introduces the second difficulty. 'Making sense' means 'making sense to us', that is, within the cognitive capacity we bring to bear. This is sharply illustrated by the desire to 'make sense' of the phenomena addressed in quantum theory by finding analogies and metaphors that will give an at least approximate grasp of what is going on. Schrodinger's cat is an analogy, 'entanglement' a metaphor. The sense-making enterprise involves bringing back to the proximal side the results achieved on the distal side and interpreting them – not translating them, in this case – into the former's conceptual resources. On the face of it this appears a harmless enterprise, but there is a respect in which it is not so. This is the constraint imposed by the canon of enquiry for fundamental science that results pass stringent empirical tests. *Physics Letters* defines a 'discovery' as what merits evaluation as Sigma 5, denoting a 0.00006 per cent chance that a variation from an expected value is merely a fluctuation.[7] (Statistical analyses of e.g. voting intentions in an electorate are satisfied with Sigma 3.) A requirement of science is that hypotheses must make testable predictions to pass muster, which places the evaluation of the test outcomes within researchers' capacities to make sense of them – consisting in (for example) what they see on dials and computer printouts in light of the theory which interprets them. The difficulty of finding ways to run empirical tests of string theory's claims is held against it; the tiny scales and massive energies involved jointly constitute a very high barrier to doing so. Some proponents of string theory argue that the beauty of the mathematics is alone sufficient to validate it. The matter is controversial, and the record of human ingenuity does not rule out the prospect of finding clever ways to do it. But while it fails to be testable, it prompts some in the physics community to regard it as 'pseudoscience'.[8]

In making testability a fundamental requirement in its canons of enquiry, science says that imagination or mere possibility is insufficient for anything aspiring to be taken seriously. This in other terms is to say that *conceivability* is required; there has to be a navigable conceptual route to follow that connects what is currently accepted in the way of theory to the proposal, its navigability consisting in the prospects of testability. The general implications of this are discussed shortly; one thing to remark immediately is that as a constraint on the epistemic aim of 'making sense' of what is embodied, proposed or

---

[7]For some results, as in the Higgs boson discovery at CERN, 5-Sigma is the 0.00003% chance that the observations were merely a statistical fluctuation in the search for data exceeding the value on one half of the normal distribution graph.

[8]One proposed test of string theory is to see whether it is consistent with cosmic expansion; if the theory of inflation in the universe's very earliest moments is correct, it falsifies string theory. D. Z. Foster, 'Will String Theory Finally Be Put to the Experimental Test?' *Scientific American*, June 2020.

implied in a discourse, a conceivability constraint anchors the aim to the proximal side of the endeavour.

'Conceivability' is a modal notion. Modality enters thinking about the world in a number of ways, the most obvious being that when we wonder how things are in a given domain, a good way to begin answering the question is, in line with the foregoing, to hypothesise how they could be and to test the hypothesis. In thinking about how they could be we restrict the possibilities. I am looking for my shoes; they could be in the cupboard or under the bed – testing in this case is going and looking in one of those places and if the shoes are not there looking in the other – but I do not include Mars among places to look. If they are not under the bed either, I might think that because they *have* to be somewhere – a form of necessity enters the picture – I extend the range of possibilities. But I still do not include Mars as one such. On what grounds? On conceivability grounds. I can imagine them there; indeed in circumstances in which a Mars landing module could transport them there, I can conceive of their being there, but an elaborate conceptual path has to be navigated to do so. 'Normal' circumstances relating to a pair of shoes I was lately wearing restrict the range of possibilities to be investigated.

This pedestrian tale is rich in implications. It illustrates the context-dependence of judgments about what is possible in a given domain, and therefore presupposes the relevant set of considerations about the nature of the domain which imposes limits on how things could be in it. The limits need not be determinate; unusual things happen (e.g. an astronaut borrowed my shoes, wore them on a mission to Mars, and left them there for some reason). When I think 'the shoes have to be somewhere' the necessity invoked is a *natural* necessity; it is not of course that the artificial kind *shoes* have by their nature as shoes to be somewhere, but because they are spatio-temporal material particulars (I will not say in this context 'physical' particulars). Such particulars have by definition to be somewhere in space and time (the previous parenthesis acknowledges that physical particulars may exist only in time). It is thus not *logical* necessity, though there is a viewpoint that imputes *metaphysical* necessity to some natural things, for a chief example natural kinds. That the shoes must be somewhere is a conditional necessity, the condition being the standard congery of facts accepted, in this case, in the scheme of perceptual experience about spatio-temporal material particulars.

In the conceptual scheme of perceptual experience, assumptions about how things generally are in the domain over which that experience ranges thus place elastic boundaries around how particular things in it can be. The interaction of concepts of practical possibility and conditional necessity in the justification of particular modal judgments made in the context of the perceptual domain (and by extension the empirical domain, but here complications arise; if restricted to the *accessible* regions of the domain then the distinction collapses[9]) consists in demarcating a range of possibilities by assuming how something has to be for that to be the range. But now note that the point generalises; delete 'practical' and lift the restriction to the domain of perceptual experience, and the statement is: the interaction of concepts of possibility and necessity in the justification of modal judgments consists in demarcating a range of possibilities by assuming how something has to be for that to be the range. A major example is that for a world to be possible it must necessarily be the case that it be internally consistent.

In giving an account of *epistemic* modality it is natural to take the case of an agent for whom some proposition is epistemically necessary just in case her evidence for asserting it, under ideal conditions of reasoning, rules out the possibility of the proposition's negation

---

[9]This point turns on what is made of *conceivability*, below.

being true. This relativises the epistemic necessity of propositions to the agents who assert them, because even under ideal conditions of reasoning other agents might have insufficient evidence to rule out the possibility of the truth of the proposition's negation. In the case of what the conceptual scheme of perceptual experience licenses as epistemically necessary, the body of shared assumptions about the domain is taken to be sufficient in the required way likewise under a *ceteris paribus* clause. Only in the case of propositions whose truth-value is determinable *a priori* is the clause dropped; hence the temptation to pair the *a priori* with both analyticity and metaphysical necessity, at least in regarding the extensions of truths known *a priori* to be coterminous with analytically true propositions and true propositions asserting metaphysical necessity. But Kant and Kripke offered reasons to resist this: for Kant there are synthetic *a priori* truths, and for Kripke there are necessary truths discoverable *a posteriori*.[10]

The cases where necessary truths are argued to be discoverable only *a posteriori*, including natural laws and relations between the mental and physical, predicate metaphysical realism for their domains. Absent this commitment, there appear to be only two domains where a concept of necessity gets traction: logical necessity, of which the paradigm is a theorem's entailment by the axioms and derivation rules of a formal system, and conditional epistemic necessity as described.

In introducing discussion of modality the concepts of possibility and necessity take centre-stage independently of their relativity to a domain of discourse. A third is mentioned: contingency. A fourth too often ignored is actuality. Employment of the concept of possible

---

[10]Immanuel Kant, *Critque of Pure Reason* in P. Guyer and A. Wood (eds.), *The Cambridge Edition of the Works of Immanuel Kant* (Cambridge University Press 1992); Saul Kripke, *Naming and Necessity* (Harvard University Press 1980). See also Hilary Putnam, *Philosophy of Logic* (Harper & Row 1971).

worlds allows a ready way of characterising each; to employ for initial purposes the terms 'proposition' and 'true', one says that a proposition is necessary if it is true in all possible worlds, is possible if it is true in at least one, and contingent if it is true in at least one but not all. One relatively minor reason why actuality tends not to figure in this schema is that to say 'a proposition is actual if__' is an inapt locution, requiring in its place a version of 'a proposition that states what is actually the case', and invites the formulation 'an actuality proposition is one that is true in the real world', shifting the burden onto the question of identifying the real world. Whereas the identity conditions of possible worlds can be given by specifying propositions taken to be true in them, the identification of what is actual has to presuppose the satisfaction of identity conditions uniquely specifying the real world. And the complication in this is by now obvious: the question of which world is the '(putatively "ultimately metaphysically") real world' is moot. The complication is compounded when one conjoins the two propositions 'the conceptual scheme (metonymously, "the world") of perceptual experience is inconsistent' and 'no inconsistent world is possible'. As has already been flagged, the way out of the dilemma is to distinguish 'actual for a domain' from the 'real' in 'ultimately real', the case for which occurs in §8.

First, though, it is important to canvass a suggestion about the role of actuality in the matrix of relations among the uncontextualised concepts of the modalities. Predicate the interdefinability of 'possibility' and 'necessity', or more economically employ one of them with negation. 'Contingently p' can be defined as 'possibly p in only a subset of all worlds'. What is actual is possible but not necessarily contingent by this definition, because what is actual might be necessary as a deity is taken to be in most theologies. The question whether there is a necessary being by this definition existing in all possible worlds does not raise a further question as to whether all worlds inhabited by a necessary being are therefore themselves necessary; in marking the distinction between necessary *being* and necessary *propositions* we admit the intelligibility of asserting that there are possible worlds inhabited by a necessary being and possible worlds in which no being is (metaphysically) necessary: 'god – though defined as a necessary being – might not exist'.

The intelligibility of the theological concept of 'necessary being' turns on the claim that the idea of a regress of contingencies without a first ground is unintelligible. The short way with this is to note that the concept of a domain of mutual contingencies is possible, as in rebuttals of the cosmological argument in the philosophy of religion, noting that the universe could be its own ground. 'Necessary being' is an arbitrary solution to the discomfort provoked by the putative threat of infinite regress, a form of conceptual housekeeping parasitic on the idea of the ultimately real. The idea is an extrapolation from that of conditional necessity, stipulating that a chosen first term for a chain of regress be treated as absolute.[11] (The fact that the choice might be motivated by other commitments arising from e.g. scriptures or

---

[11]This is an artefact of language: the appearance of intelligibility arises from the ease with which negation is applied. If an expression makes sense, its negation is taken to make sense. We know alas what it is to be mortal, imperfect and finite, and by negating the terms think we know what it is to be immortal, perfect and infinite. Given the recursive nature of language (iterations of conjunctions offer an infinite number of grammatically well-formed expressions), what can be said outruns what can be thought. 'I can trisect a Euclidean plane angle using only ruler and compass' is an intelligible remark that nevertheless states a logical impossibility. The commission of category mistakes is another product of grammar. This, incidentally, is why Ryle's 'polar concept' argument against scepticism does not work; conceptual polarities can be such that one concept can be intelligible because, say, applicable and its 'opposite', produced by negation, only seemingly-intelligible, as in the polarity 'mortal-immortal'. Ryle argued against the sceptic that because we at least sometimes know what it is to be wrong we must therefore at least sometimes know what it is to be right. G. Ryle, *Dilemmas* (Cambridge University Press 1960); A. C. Grayling, *The Refutation of Scepticism* (Duckworth 1976).

traditions, and therefore non-arbitrary in that sense, does not render it non-arbitrary in the germane sense.)

These thoughts form a significant part of what is required for analysing the concept of 'metaphysical necessity' as such, given that deity is offered as the prime example of something that must exist, cannot not exist, exists without contingency on anything apart from itself, and is thereby (a separate thought) the absolute ground for anything else that exists, serving as both an ontological and explanatory terminus. Whether any other candidate for necessary being has this last property is a matter for the case that is offered for its necessary existence; in the case of deity the move from the thought that 'anything that exists must have a ground of existence' (a conditional Principle of Sufficient Reason) to 'there is an absolute ground of existence' is illegitimate without supplementary premises, so it would be well for a general conception of 'necessary existence' that it be decoupled from it and explicated independently of its role in explaining contingent existence. But this turns out to be hard to do, for it is hard to explicate necessary existence without making it parasitic on its contrast to contingent existence; and this at the very least threatens to evacuate it of content.

Indeed, it arguably does more; for a polar-concept consideration looms. We know what it is for a state of affairs to be contingent – dependent for its existence and character on some other state of affairs, which makes sense of 'conditionally necessary' (as in nomological necessity in the laws of physics) – but our grip on 'absolutely necessary' goes only via 'non-contingent'. The move made in such cases turns on the implicit analogy with cases where both poles of a conceptual polarity require the other, as in 'empty-full', but in these cases there are independent ways of grasping the sense of either concept without invoking the other. Relative polarities ('short-tall') require a third term, viz. a metric of comparison. Alarm bells ring when one pole has a sense graspable independently of the other, but the other can only be defined by negation on the independently graspable sense.

Candidates offered for non-divine necessary existence include numbers and possible worlds themselves. The idea that numbers are necessary existents introduces the more general idea that some abstracta exist necessarily; this and the idea that it is necessary that there are possible worlds in addition to the actual world is considered below in connection with actuality and conceivability. But the point being approached by these considerations is that the concept of metaphysical necessity requires realism for the domain in which metaphysical necessities occur, and the question is whether this can be made out.

Along with questioning the idea of 'necessary being' one can for present purposes set aside that of 'logical necessity' by noting that, in its use for explicating deducibility and entailment, it is in fact a form of conditional necessity, in that what counts as a theorem is contingent on the axioms, definitions and derivation rules of the formal system in which it occurs. The notion of *absolute* logical necessity, if there is one, requires – on analogy with the 'necessary being' case – that there be some irreducible foundational logical law or laws upon which *any* formal system rests. Aristotle doubtless thought that the 'laws of thought' (contradiction, excluded middle and identity, *pace* the equivalence of the first two by De Morgan's Theorem) provided such a basis. One need only invoke alternative logics (e.g. non-bivalent logics) and problems with 'identity' in applications to reasoning about contingent matters to destabilise the thought that logic has absolute foundations outside the needs of reasoning about specified subject-matters, whose content is what motivates the choice of logic for them. For example an intuitionistic logic, dispensing with excluded middle, appears apt for quantum theory.

Turn attention to epistemic modality. Here – unsurprisingly in light of the base case for ontological considerations being perceptual experience – we find that actuality is the fundamental modality. To explain why some state of affairs is regarded as possible, we invoke the consideration that nothing known blocks (stands in the way of) its being actual. To say that a state of affairs is contingent is to say that its actuality is dependent on other states of affairs being actual. To derive the concept of conditional necessity we take the further step of saying that for anything possible to be actual its being so requires some relevant other thing to be actual, formulable as 'X is conditionally necessary for Y iff, if Y is actual, then (a) X is actual and (b) X is an indispensable ground of Y'. Counterfactuals, statements of natural laws, accounts of dispositional properties and the logic of transcendental arguments draw upon the concept of conditionality in this sense, and take the logical form of biconditional statements accordingly.

To derive the concept of absolute necessity a different step has to be taken, though it is not immediately clear what it is. To try saying, for example, that something is absolutely necessary if it is actual in every possible state of affairs and that its being so is a condition of their possibility is to universalise conditionality, not to absolutise necessity. But in any case it falls foul of the idea that it is possible that everything about a possible state of affairs is contingent. In seeking a justification for a principle to the effect that anything whatever, X, must ultimately have an absolutely necessary ground, the obvious resource is to say that explanatory and causal regresses must have a first term at risk of the unintelligibility of X. But this does not solve the problem, for it is in effect itself a statement of conditional necessity – viz. for the intelligibility of X – disguised by remoteness, and moves the unintelligibility risk to the concepts of an inexplicable or uncaused first term. It is hard to see what other resources there are for making the concept out.

It is by way of the 'nothing known stands in the way' condition on epistemic possibility that the concept of the modal 'conceivability' enters. And it is here that a major objection appears immediately to arise, namely, that the implication of these thoughts is an unacceptable conflation of the notions of possibility and conceivability, which cannot be right given that the extension of 'possible' is far greater than the extension of 'conceivable'. This is based on two different points, though it is natural to conjoin them, one definitional and one empirical.

The first is that a defining characteristic of epistemic possibility (as with possibility *tout court*) is the absence of inconsistency. This point needs qualification; 'absence of inconsistency' is only a necessary, not a sufficient, condition for epistemic possibility, given that a fairy tale can be internally consistent, but much stands in the way of its constituting an actual state of affairs. The factors that stand in the way are determined by the canons of enquiry at work in the conceptual scheme embodied in the discourse of perceptual experience, these being what identify which items in the ontology projected by the discourse are to count as actual.

The empirical point is that many things once unconceived are now conceived and were therefore possible. The temptation to say 'once inconceivable' is resisted as a mere *façon de parler*, because they turned out to be conceived; it means that the materials available for its conception were at the given point unavailable; it was inconceivable only relative to the epistemic situation – the absence of information or vocabulary enabling conception of it. By definition nothing can be known to be inconceivable beyond recognition *that* some state of affairs whose description contains a contradiction is so.[12] Entertaining the thought that there are inconceivable things by inference from the

---

[12]One knows that it is *inconceivable* that a Euclidean plane angle can be trisected with ruler and compass alone. One can, in a sense, *imagine* this being done – perhaps the geometer at work in that Vermeer painting is doing it – but only by not witnessing the putative procedure itself.

finite cognitive powers of humans relativises the former to the latter, and has the same extension as 'yet unconceived', viz. the complement class of everything so far conceived. The senses of the expressions differ, 'inconceivable' having a more committal sense than 'yet unconceived', but whereas the sense of the latter can be grasped through the history of concept development, it is unclear what provides grasp of the former other than the seeming-meaningfulness achieved by negation on 'conceivable'.

But in any case maintaining the distinction between possibility and conceivability is crucial to the epistemic enterprise itself. Enquiry is enquiry into the question whether anything blocks some state of affairs from being actual. It involves making something conceivable, including and often by creating concepts which extend, refine or displace concepts held antecedently to a given stage of enquiry. Commitment to the idea that the extension of 'possible' outruns that of 'conceivable' is at very least a strategic commitment of enquiry, turning on the 'nothing blocks' point – more accurately, 'nothing yet blocks' – because one major form of discovery is precisely that this is so.

By conceivability is meant forming concepts, and doing this consists in mapping a route into a field of possibilities itself demarcated by the absence at the epistemic starting point of what stands in the way of being actual. Relativisation to context is accordingly indispensable; even creative leaps in science have reference to the subject matter to be explained or at least illuminated by the endeavour, thus prompting it. Enquiry aims and often succeeds in bringing into view what was not hitherto conceived, in good outcomes demonstrating that nothing stands in the way of further possibilities (further revelations about what is actual), thereby providing the next epistemic starting point. But if what is proposed as a topic for enquiry is detached from anything that can be identified either as its point or its starting point,

     The Metaphysics of Experience

it is hard to see what to make of it. It is a datum that some imaginings – the fictions of Jules Verne about submarines and moon landings are cases in point – can prompt conceivings of ways in which they could become or even just be actual, but that is because the chain of conditionals linking the idea to its realisation (think of what a Victorian marine engineer might have listed as the problems to be overcome in building a submarine) specify successive contingencies, among the earliest being 'what nothing blocks from being actual' at that point.

Descartes distinguished imaginability from conceivability by saying that he could conceive of the difference between a chiliagon and a 998-sided figure, but could not imagine it. He was trading on his period's conflation of imagining and envisioning (imagining as forming an image; literally, a mental picture). One can imagine – form a mental image of – (say) a hippogryph, by picturing a winged creature whose front half is an eagle and rear half is a horse. On a Cartesian view of the matter, such a creature would appear to be imaginable but inconceivable; in the coming state of genetic science matters might be otherwise. It remains that, despite this, the example points up the ease of imagining a hippogryph in contrast to conceiving of the steps required to engineer it genetically. But in any case the forming of mental images is not a necessary condition for imagining; the imaging connotation in Descartes is too restrictive. The literature of science fiction might prompt different, or no, images in readers' minds, and bring to imagination unpicturable states of affairs which operate as (as it were) pretend conceptions. And some of these might turn out to suggest actually conceivable ones, which is where the health and value of imagining resides. This is a point for the *psychology* of enquiry (the familiar example comes to mind of Kukulé's ourobouros dream prompting the idea of carbon atoms in benzene forming a ring); for the *methodology* of enquiry, conceivability is a condition of any next steps in the process.[13]

The principal reason for scepticism about the constraint represented by conceivability is the background commitment to realism about the unknown hinterland of any state of knowledge. Such hinterlands are rich in possibilities, some of which will be brought into the realm of actuality by discovery; by extrapolation from the unactualised possibilities one can formulate the proposition that a realm not just of yet unactualised but unactualisable possibilities stretches into the distance; this by courtesy of language (grammatically well-formed sentences can state what is impossible, e.g. the 'Euclidean plane angle trisection' example, or nonsensical, e.g. 'green ideas sleep furiously'). From the practical point of view the distinction makes no difference. It is enough in either case that there is an exciting realm of ignorance to be explored.

From a philosophical point of view, however, there is a large difference, and one that underwrites commitments to metaphysical realism. The idea is not arbitrary, in at least the sense that ways have been offered of motivating the idea that the realm of ignorance contains inconceivable and therefore, from that standpoint, unactualisable possibilities, which is what a realist commitment to the domain appears to license. The challenge for a defender of such a view is to show that it is genuinely intelligible, as opposed merely to seeming so, that with respect to some domain (or 'the world' as a whole) we can have an 'absolute' or 'objective' conception of it that is altogether independent of conceivability constraints.

---

[13]In the offing, Popper's remark about constraints on theoretical explanation: 'a theory that explains everything explains nothing', a logical terminus of the falsification thesis. K. Popper, *The Logic of Scientific Discovery* (Routledge 2002).

An argument to this effect is offered by McGinn.[14] I comment on it as illustrative of the kind of considerations that might be invoked in its favour.

The aim in McGinn's account is to provide what Nagel calls 'objective transcendence', a view from nowhere, unconditioned by facts about subjective aspects of perceptual experience such as those necessitating consideration of secondary qualities and indexicality. The nub of the argument is that we (humans) are constitutionally incapable of escaping our ignorance about regions of reality which transcend our cognitive capacities. As McGinn puts it, 'The limits of our minds are ... not the limits of reality. It is deplorably anthropocentric to insist that reality be constrained by what the human mind can conceive.'[15] So when regions of reality 'elude our cognitive grasp' this is no reason for taking it that reference to them is empty. His case turns on a notion of 'cognitive closure'. A type of mind is cognitively closed with respect to some domain if and only if concept-forming procedures available to that type of mind cannot give it access to the domain. Minds come in different kinds; monkeys can conceive of things rats cannot conceive, humans can conceive of things monkeys cannot conceive.[16] A good example of closure, McGinn argues, is provided by the perceptual case; some creatures (bees, butterflies, dogs) can access ranges of the electro-magnetic spectrum that humans cannot, an empirically ascertainable datum.

---

[14] Colin McGinn, *The Subjective View* (Oxford University Press 1983) and 'Can We Solve the Mind-Body Problem' *Mind* 98 (1989). In the close offing, Thomas Nagel, *The View from Nowhere* (Oxford University Press 1986). McGinn offered two attempts to establish his conclusion; I discuss both in 'On How Not to Be Realistic' in *Truth, Meaning and Realism* 2007, but here concentrate on the second and later one, drawing on that discussion. Among the reasons for dispensing with the first is that it turns on a mistaken conflation of idealism and anti-realism: see §1 above and Grayling, 'Understanding Realism' in *Truth, Meaning and Realism* 2007.

[15] McGinn, *Can We Solve the Mind-Body Problem*, 366.

[16] Ibid., 350.

'But such closure does not reflect adversely on the reality of the properties that lie outside the representational capacities in question; a property is no less real for not being reachable from a certain kind of perceiving and conceiving mind'.[17]

The first major problem lies in taking limitations on what is perceivable to underwrite an inference to limitations on what is conceivable (obviously, the existence of ranges of the electromagnetic spectrum accessible by butterflies is not inconceivable). McGinn's argument relies on the inference to motivate a much stronger claim, that an extrapolation from facts about the contrast between what monkeys and humans can conceive to the claim that there must (note the modality) be things human cannot (note the modality) conceive. On McGinn's view, by parity of reasoning from the perceptual case we can entertain the idea that there could be things conceived by minds as superior to human minds as human minds are to monkey minds. McGinn illustrates the move by offering the conjunction of these propositions: 'there is some property of the brain that accounts naturalistically for consciousness' and 'we are cognitively closed to that property'.[18] Leave aside the question whether neuropsychology shares the pessimism of the latter remark, and focus upon the fact that perceptual closure does not entail cognitive closure, the move required for taking it that its being imaginable that there are inconceivable facts to its being conceivable that there are such facts – a large jump in itself, and not yet a substantiation of the claim that there are such facts.

The move has two phases. In the first, we acknowledge that humans know things monkeys do not know, and that monkeys cannot know those things. The second phase consists in the claim that, by analogy,

---

[17]Ibid., 351.
[18]Ibid., 351–52.

there are things humans not only do not but cannot know. As this is an unverifiable empirical claim it has to be treated as an *a priori* principle supported by the first phase consideration. The indisputable weaker claim, that there are things humans do not know, is a plausible target as conclusion for the argument. But in taking it to entail that there must be things we cannot know McGinn makes a claim stronger even than metaphysical realism requires, for it is not just an existential claim about realms of fact transcending a temporally located limitation on our cognitive capacities. If the stronger claim appears *prima facie* plausible, one has to ask what its plausibility relies upon. The answer is: upon its being imaginable. The question whether being able to imagine something as inconceivable licenses treating it as actually so is answered in the foregoing argument in the negative.

McGinn's 'different levels' analogy in fact subverts the ambition of his argument. It introduces the idea of an epistemic agency better-placed than humans by analogy with the better-placed epistemic capacities of humans compared to monkeys. But this relativises the argument in a way that reintroduces conceivability as a constraint: we explain the inconceivability of a realm of fact by humans in relation to its conceivability by (imagined) better-equipped cognisers, but this claim is not that there are inconceivable facts *tout court* (if superior cognisers existed the facts would be conceivable for them) but only that they are inconceivable *by us*. In going beyond the indisputable consideration that there are things that are inconceivable in the present state of knowledge to the strong claim that *there are* realms of fact in principle unknowable, the large jump made is not sustained by the analogies offered.

The strategic value of leaving it open that there is much that is unknown lies in its encouragement to enquiry. The commitment to conducting enquiry by striving to attain an objective ideal standpoint is in this way interpretable as regulative; it is the same as what in another guise is framed as seeking convergence on truth. The regulative idea that there must be a truth about a domain is what motivates commitment to realism about the domain. But then this shows realism itself to be a regulative commitment. To assume a realist attitude to a domain is not the same thing as proving the truth of realism. Tucked away in arguments such as McGinn's one suspects that a *petitio principii* to that effect lurks.

The tenour of these considerations is that it is not just that a realist commitment, understood as strategic and regulative, is all that is needed in the case of perceptual experience, but that if understanding the discourse of perceptual experience is assimilated to understanding discourse in general, then realist commitments in other discourses are likewise strategic, appropriately relativized to the domains in question. Taking realism *literally* rather than strategically is a motive for treating the concepts of truth, reference and modality univocally for all domains, and that is the source of philosophical difficulties that doing so generates. This is the key claim of the argument in this account; to summarise §§3 and 4, in this standpoint reference goes via descriptions, truth is a number of substantive properties contextualised to the canons of enquiry for a domain, modality is conditional, and reduction, aimed at explanation in the ideal and clarification, illumination and suggestion otherwise – all valuable outcomes when they potentiate enquiry and, where relevant, control of phenomena referred to in reduced discourses – is often incomplete.

The suggestion that realist commitments to domains are strategic in all cases and is regulative for enquiry in them requires further examination, along with the proposed distinction between 'real' and 'actual', and the implication of this for the concept of 'deferral' left pending in relation to 'ultimate reality' and the prospects for metaphysical realism. This is the topic of the next and final section.

§8

Reality and Deferral

For the purposes of the discussion in this section the term *realism* is distinguished from the term *metaphysical realism* and each given specific senses. In discussions involving the former term's application in the context of a given domain it is taken that it is or is related via reductions to what is implied by the latter term. The discussion here gives grounds for holding apart domain-contextualised realist commitments from the idea of ultimate general reality defined shortly, and by explicating the connection between them showing why the latter is intrinsically *deferrable* in the sense to be explained.

Realism denotes a double commitment: to the existence, in a domain of discourse, of the referents of that discourse's referring terms, and to their existence's independence of the cognitive capacities and activity of the discoursers.

The expression *metaphysical realism* denotes the strong thesis that there is an ultimate general reality, *ultimate* in being itself irreducible to any other, and causally and explanatorily final with respect to itself and all domains reducible to it.

Realism about a domain neither entails nor requires that the items in it which exist independently of discoursers' cognitive powers do so in a way that transcends those powers *absolutely*. If something is conceivable within the domain its being so *ipso facto* brings it within discoursers' cognitive powers. Moreover there is every reason to take it that there is plenty about the domains of perceptual experience and science (both natural and social, the latter including history) which is not or not yet known, but which could come to be known and are anyway conceivable or may become so as concepts are developed in the processes of enquiry. 'Existing independently of discoursers' cognitive powers' means that acts of cognition do not cause or bring into existence their targets, and does not without supplement imply anything further. To claim that they could or must exist not merely unknown but unknowable requires the kind of claims that, in §7, were argued to amount at best to a case of *imagining* that it is conceivable that this is so. It is conceivable that a domain of what underlies perceptual experience and science could exist and have the character it does even if no cognisers of any kind existed; that is a different point, but one often conflated with the idea of facts about the domains of perceptual experience and science transcending cognisers' powers absolutely, which is a claim about cognisers, not about the domain and its contents. To see why, consider that the envisaged possibility does not by itself rule out that if there were cognisers they would cognise the domain; a different argument to the effect that there is or (more weakly) could be a domain uncognisable *tout court* would be needed to establish that even if there were cognisers of *any* kind the domain would be inaccessible to them – necessarily uncognisable. It is hard to see what such an argument would look like.

This is also not what is at stake in regard to metaphysical realism, for the idea of a causally and explanatorily ultimate reality is not by itself the idea of an uncognisable reality. Metaphysical realism does not entail or require, for the same reasons as apply to realism for a domain, that ultimate general reality be intrinsically unknowable. For this the same separate case has to be made which is better than merely imagining that it could be thus. Imagining this is prompted by the fact of discoursers' finite powers coupled with extrapolations from the analogy of the levels of cognitive capacity between humans and creatures thought to be of lesser intellectual capacity in at least those respects that humans possess it. The comparison looks suggestive, and accordingly offers itself as underwriting the intelligibility of the claim that there could be greater powers than humans possess; insofar as this is a case of considering how it would be if the powers humans in fact possess were potentiated (as indeed they are by instrumental means: telescopes and the rest), this counts as conceivability. But it still falls short of substantiating a claim that *there are* facts intrinsically unknowable or inconceivable by any cognitive agency.

The characterisations given of both realism for a domain and metaphysical realism require qualification, for they are presented from a realist point of view, up to now ignoring the point that the conceptual schemes of perceptual experience and science themselves have constitutive roles in relation to the domains they address. Recall the point in §1 that a realist attitude to a domain predicates the hybridity of the relations between it and discoursers, *internal* in the direction *discourser to domain* on broad content grounds, *external* in the direction *domain to discourser* on the ground that the domain is not existentially dependent on the discourser's cognitive activities. Yet by its nature discourse about a domain is contingent upon discoursers' cognitive capacities, embodies the conceptual scheme they constitute, and projects the ontology the scheme articulates. This is the consideration that motivates an anti-realist attitude to the domain. The appearance of a direct conflict between realist and anti-realist attitudes arises from taking the anti-realist point to amount to a consequential claim about the domain's ontology, namely, that its constituents are existentially dependent on discoursers' cognitive activities – in short, are created by them. On the definition of 'realism' in the second paragraph of this section, this appears plainly to be the implication. But the appearance vanishes upon enrichment of the respective points being made. As the argument below makes out more fully, in the realist commitment the independence from discoursers of the referents in their discourse is existential, that is, metaphysical for the domain in the sense that the existence of the referents is finally underwritten by reference to metaphysical realism. In the anti-realist commitment the dependence on discourse of the referents is *epistemological* not metaphysical. Recognition of this dissolves the apparent contradiction between the standpoints.

The realist might in fact be willing to concede the latter point with respect to the domain of perceptual discourse, moving her metaphysical commitment to the referents of terms in the science that explains how perceptual experience arises, and from what. Prompted by the consideration that these in their turn are projections from the discourse that organises experience at that level, the next step is to move the commitment to an assumed fundamental level, no longer a commitment to an existential independence from activities of cognition in a discourse, but to metaphysical realism as such.

In what follows an intuitive understanding of what is meant by the coined term 'actuals' is being assumed – denoting what are pretheoretically termed 'real things' (for the domain) and sorted from the discourse's total ontology of referents by systematic epistemological considerations. A little more detail about the concept of what is actual in the ontology of a domain brings into view a consideration made interesting by the overall argument here. This concerns the discourse of the domain of social experience, 'social reality', a domain not just as of great importance to the quotidian experience of discoursers as the spatio-temporal domain but arguably even more so in some respects.

The realist assumption is powerful and apt for organising discourses of the perceptual and scientific domains – a fact which is itself a driver to treating it literally in these cases – but although it operates in other domains, not least in that of social experience, it does not tempt in the same way. Few would claim that the institution 'the United States Congress' has the same actuality or at least *kind* of actuality as a grizzly bear. Challenged for a reason, a respondent might say that bears are natural entities produced by evolutionary forces whereas Congress is instituted by agreement among people, an artefact of social interactions. Perhaps there are intermediate categories of assurance about whether a referent exists in ways more like the existence of Congress than the existence of bears; psychological properties perhaps, deferred to neurological properties such that the terms for referents of psychological discourse are therefore treated as *façons de parler* which, in a completed neuroscience, would drop out of use just as 'demon possession' dropped out of use in psychiatry. On such a view, structures of the brain and events in them count with bears as actuals, such referents as 'dream', 'anxiety attack', 'memory' as shorthand for them, while remaining actuals for the domain of (perhaps 'folk') psychological discourse.

There is, however, something temporising about withholding the same degree of actuality to Congress as to grizzly bears. Consider the properties whose possession identifies something as an actual – a 'real thing' – in the domain of perceptual experience. It can be sensorily encountered, it enters into causal relations with other such things, it occupies a space roughly equivalent to its own volume and configuration exclusively of other things and has some degree at least of temporal duration, or if it is an event it occurs in or over a space and likewise has a temporal duration of some extent; it is robust in resisting alteration and displacement unless by something with a robustness of its own sufficient to effect this, e.g. through the exercise of kinetic energy, and – a crucial component – it is publicly available for encounter by more than one perceiver at a time and, reidentifiably, over time. It is by detection of such properties that items in the ontology of perceptual experience are selected as actual.

The elements of their haecceity shared by Congress are: being fundamentally encounterable by the means suitable to encountering them, publicly available to more than one encounterer, causally connected via the environment it occupies (both as a cause and an effect) to the nature and activity of other things, robust and correlatively resistant to anything insufficiently robust itself to overcome its resistance, and relatively enduring. It is evident from this that socially constituted entities are actual in the domain of social experience by possession of much the same properties as naturally evolved actuals in the domain of perceptual experience.

The purpose of pointing this out is to illuminate further the notions of 'actuals' and ontology-projection by a discourse, while granting the differences. The chief of these is that in the domain of social experience decisions about what is actual are not as straightforward as in the perceptual case, because they are more dependent on a supervening level of selection, this time for the criteria for selecting, in turn, what is to count as actual. For example, are witches actual? If there are such things as supernatural powers, spells effected by incantations and potions concocted from 'eye of newt and toe of frog' whose consumption result in people becoming kings or falling in love, and if there are people with practical ability in casting effective such spells and concocting effective such potions, the term 'witch' would denote an actual in the social domain. Whereas *belief* in witches is actual (the belief being causal, resistant, encounterable etc. – tragically so in history, and today in some parts of the world, for people believed to be witches), it is less persuasive that *witches* as such are so. Granting this, it remains that institutions that have the standing in the public eye of Congress or the Marine Corps are as haecceitous as grizzly bears; encountering them in certain ways can be as consequential as encountering a hungry grizzly bear. Their claim to be actuals in their domain is indisputable. Therefore although it can be argued that achieving actuality in the social domain is harder than achieving it in the perceptual domain, the parallels sustain the general point: an actual in a domain is determined by the epistemology for the domain, and this is the point to be carried.

To fill out the considerations about 'realism' and 'metaphysical realism' implied by the application of each and their connections, one must retrace steps.

The relation of *realism* about a reducible domain to *metaphysical realism* predicates the idea of the reducibility of all reducible domains to a single ultimately existing domain, even if indirectly. An assumption to the effect that realism about a domain acquires its content from that relation underlies commitment to taking it that the existence and independence from cognition of the actuals in its discourse are owed to eventual dependence upon or derivation from ultimate reality. This is so even in cases of incomplete reductions; the idea that emergent or supervenient properties are ultimately inexplicable is conceptually intolerable, and is in turn itself a driver to the assumption of an ultimately and irreducibly final reality, understanding which will embrace what is left over in incomplete reductions.

In foregoing sections a distinction was made between the ontology of a domain – the inventory of everything referred to in it – and the subset of that inventory regarded as actual. Decisions about what referents are actual ('actually exist') and those which do not are made by the canons of enquiry for the domain. For example, the property of whiteness is referred to in the domain of perceptual experience, and a familiar traditional debate surrounds the question of whether *whiteness* should be regarded nominalistically or realistically. In its simplest form the disagreement turns on whether one should commit to there being an entity, *whiteness*, which its instances (white surfaces) instantiate or in which they participate,[1] or whether one should regard 'whiteness' as a general term of convenience collecting what is similar about individual patches of white and, though the name of a property, nevertheless not denoting something existing in addition to its instances. The epistemology of perceptual experience persuasively inclines to treating white patches as actual and the universal *whiteness* as non-actual (nominal). On these distinctions, both '(this) white patch' and 'whiteness' are referring terms; both individual white surfaces and the property of whiteness are in the ontology of perceptual experience, but only the former are actual.[2]

In this terminology 'real' and 'actual' are not synonyms; whiteness is a real property – it exists; there is such a thing in the perceptual domain as whiteness, nominalistically conceived, but the universal *whiteness* is not itself actual, only its instances are.

The twofold claim to be made out in this section is that realism *about a domain* is a strategically significant commitment, an assumption of the epistemological framework taken to be undischargeable for discourse about the domain in order for it to make sense.[3] A significant distinction arises between those discourses which are regarded as reducible and those that are not, and what this implies for an eventuating commitment to metaphysical realism. The discourse of perceptual experience is regarded as reducible, because the actual referents of its referring terms are regarded as entities and events whose

---

[1] Cf Plato, *Parmenides* and the Medieval realist-nominalist debate: see e.g. N. Kretzmann, A. Kenny and J. Pinborg (eds.), *The Cambridge History of Later Medieval Philosophy* (Cambridge University Press 1982).

[2] In the offing, Gilbert Ryle, 'Systematically Misleading Expressions' *Proceedings of the Aristotelian Society* 32 (1932).

[3] In the offing, Wittgenstein's 'hinge' conception in *On Certainty*, G. E. M. Anscombe and G. H. von Wright (eds.), G. E. M. Anscombe and D. Paul (trans.) (Blackwell 1969).

nature is explicable in terms of actual entities and events referred to in reducing discourses of science. By contrast, the domain of fiction is by definition one in which realist commitments are understood as being only *as if* made, though almost invariably parasitic for their sense on the discourses of perceptual and psychological domains. Disputes about other domains – the mathematical and moral, for prime examples – turn in effect on the question whether the qualifying *as if* should be dispensed with, that is, whether the entities referred to are actuals. In the case of mathematics (and putatively at least some other abstracta) if the qualifier is dispensed with, the referents (granting that some mathematical structures can be reduced to others, i.e. expressed in terms of other structures) would be candidates for metaphysically reality. In the case of moral properties it is not clear whether and if so what reducing discourse is implied if the qualifier is dropped – perhaps the discourse of psychology, or a discourse about the attitudes and commands of a deity. (This latter species of move is illustrative, as will appear, about moves to a desired absolute ground in general.)

It is here that a concept of deference invites itself. I define it operationally, as follows. A realistic attitude to reducible domains is a *deferred* commitment because asking whether realism is true of the domain or not is not the right question for the domain. In the domains of perceptual experience and the sciences a realist attitude to the referents determined by the canons of enquiry as actual is necessary for discourse about those domains to make sense; the assumption of realism for the domain is undischargeable. An assumption's being undischargeable does not make it true, it makes it conditionally necessary to be *taken to be true* (*assertible* on the theory espoused here that '_is true' is assertible-in-a-domain), and individual propositions asserted in light of it presuppose this.[4] The deferral of realism about the domain consist in the right response to the question, 'Is realism about the actuals in the domain true?' being 'It has to be assumed to be so, in order for thought and talk about them to make sense'. An illustrative comparison is the status of Wittgenstein's 'hinge' propositions in *On Certainty*, required for keying a region of discourse.

But in the offing of accepting realism for a domain is the thought that the idea itself is non-arbitrary, that an account can be given for why it performs the sense-making function successfully. Its doing so is immediate justification enough, but other sense-making assumptions might also achieve this, though at the cost of accepting less intuitive or plausible-seeming considerations in the offing. An example is Berkeley's explanation for realism about the domain of perceptual experience, namely, that the independence from discoursers of the referents to actuals in perceptual discourse consists in their being caused in discoursers' consciousness by a universal mind separate from theirs.[5] In his account an explicit reduction to a metaphysical ground (for him, the being and activity of a deity, for which he tries to provide independent proof) is offered. In contemporary

---

[4] In the offing, Strawson and Pears on presuppositional implication: 'p has a truth value iff a presupposed q is true'. P. Strawson, 'Identifying Reference and Truth-Values', *Theoria* 30 (1964): 96–118, reprinted in *Logico-linguistic Papers* (Methuen 1974) 75–95; D. Pears, 'Is Existence a Predicate?' in P. Strawson (ed.) *Philosophical Logic: Oxford Readings in Philosophy* (Oxford University Press 1967).

[5] See Grayling, *Berkeley: The Central Arguments* (Duckworth 1986). The distinction Berkeley draws between epistemological realism from the finitary point of view and the idealistic metaphysical ground of reality – to use terminology more current – is generally overlooked. His argument turns on separating the phenomenological level of the basic data of sensory experience from the phenomenal level of ordinary everyday objects and both from the metaphysical level which provides the ultimate framework of explanation for what is happening at those levels. In his terminology identification of the first and third levels is the product of 'a strict and speculative' ('philosophical') examination, to be contrasted with the 'received opinions', 'use' and 'custom' of ordinary ('vulgar') ways of talking about everyday phenomena. Time, causality and material particulars are concepts of the 'vulgar' level.

debates about realism in perceptual and scientific discourses, the notion of a reduction or successive reductions, by however remote or indirect a chain, to an ultimate metaphysical ground, hangs as it were in the background, undefined and inexplicitly (cf. the case for mathematical realism) connected to realism for the given domain. Given the independent implausibility of the notion of deity, or the even vaguer notion of an 'Absolute', or invocation of consciousness as some such ground, as candidates for 'ultimate reality', this is unsurprising; the unacceptability of traditional candidates exposes the notion outright to questions of what such a candidate might be.

A parallel deferrability applies to denotata of referring terms within a discourse when these are likewise strategic for an enquiry into some aspect of its domain. Consider for example the denotatum of the term 'neutron'. In nuclear physics this is a summative term, under a theoretical description, for three valence quarks, just as 'chair' is a summative term, under a description, for the molecules of wood and other materials constituting a chair. In the theory of the electrostatic and strong nuclear forces the denotata of 'neutron' and 'proton' are treated as individuable entities carrying, respectively, no charge and positive charge, such that the relations between them (the strong force overcoming the electrostatic repulsion between protons) can be mapped and measured. In the descending threefold hierarchy 'nucleus, hadrons, quarks and gluons' what is referred to by the first two terms can be treated, relative to certain purposes, 'as if' they are, though composite, self-subsistent unitary entities, as 'chair' is treated as denoting a self-subsistent unitary entity for most purposes. Thus the question 'is a neutron a self-subsistent unitary entity' is deferrable to the theory of quarks and their various properties. The question whether these in turn are 'truly' *elementary* is itself debated in connection with the completeness of the Standard Model. For many purposes of atomic theory in the Standard Model the deferrability even of concepts of elementary particles is on the table. Proposals to the effect that elementary particles are themselves to be accounted for by theories of strings or quantum fields indicate this, and the assumption is that reductions of discourse about these in turn must terminate ('must' terminate) in a discourse consisting in ultimate or final non-deferrable terms.[6] Even so, this conclusive step does not by itself require a commitment to metaphysical realism, because the ultimacy invoked is relative to the discourse; but in the aspiration of fundamental physics it is metaphysical reality as such that is sought – as it were, *ultimate* ultimacy, a consideration typically unexpressed because taken for granted.

Deference as applied to aspects of (to actual referents in the discourse of) a domain is in effect the postponement of questions to which, at the given level and for the purposes of the enquiry in hand, it is assumed that answers that make sense of the enquiry have already been given. Asking *those* questions makes no difference to the enquiry itself. The idea that a discourse is reducible is the idea that the discourse is deferrable as a whole.

---

[6]That the terms 'neutron' and 'proton' are conveniences for nuclear theory is demonstrated by the fact that though the operation of the strong force is more fully explained by the relation of up and down quarks (one up two down for neutrons, two up and one down for protons) constituting them, yielding among other things the theory of beta decay in which a neutron can convert into all three of a proton, an electron and an electron anti-neutrino, nevertheless such assertions as that the strong force operates over the tiny distance of 10^{-15}m (the diameter of a proton) is expressible by reference to them alone. '*Elementary* particle' denotes a particle taken to be non-composite, though in enquiry into problems with the Standard Model arguments are offered e.g. to the effect that massive quarks and leptons are not elementary; see H. C. Ottinger, 'Elementary Particles with Zero Spin Must Be Massless' *ArXiv* Physics (arXiv:2401.17344), January 2024, https://arxiv.org/abs/2401.17344#:~:text=We%20present%20an%20ontological%20argument,model%20cannot%20be%20elementary%20particles (accessed 11 March 2024). If correct, these terms accordingly also bear the same relationship to more fundamental entities that 'furniture' does to 'chair' or 'chair' to molecules of wood (etc.).

And this is the clue to metaphysical realism. The concept of metaphysical reality is an *intrinsically* deferred concept – not deferred to anything other than itself; it is by definition irreducible. Does this make the concept empty? The answer is No, because it has a *use*; the motivation for assuming that there is a causally and explanatorily ultimate reality has the organising function in thought of a frame – a frame of frames, so to say; the ultimate hinge. It is what makes realism *for a domain* intelligible as *realism* for a domain. By parity with the case of the question, 'Is realism about the actuals in the domain true?' to which the right response is, 'It has to be assumed to be so, in order for thought and talk about them to make sense', the right response to the question, 'Is there an ultimate general reality' is, 'It has to be assumed that there is, to make sense of realist commitments in domains where these are made'. As with assuming realism for a domain, the thought is non-arbitrary; the framework-providing role is what makes this so. The essential deferability of metaphysical realism consists in the absence of candidates for what it itself consists in; the failure of such candidates as an 'Absolute' or a 'deity' resides in trying to defer the idea of an ultimate metaphysical ground to something which appears to require a further such ground itself – a postponement of the problem, a sweeping under one or another carpet of concepts themselves crying out for explication. On the view taken here, what is to be said is that the *concept* of an ultimate metaphysical ground plays a role – and the role it plays is *epistemological*, concerning the epistemology of the senses of expressions in discourses; giving meaning to the terms that occur in them.

These thoughts are illuminated by inspecting what is going wrong in a debate exactly pertinent to the considerations here. As noted in §1, realism about the actuals in the domain of perceptual experience turned on an implicit acceptance of naïve realism about them, at least until advances in quantum theory and neuropsychology made philosophical discussion quietly abandon discussion in this vein. The realism in question was otherwise as it is described here: as expressing the idea that the relations in which thought, talk and experience (discourse) of the world of perceptual experience consist are external: that the world and its natural furniture could and would exist even if it had never been a relatum in such relations. This is what motivates the idea of the *independence* from discourse about it as *existential*, hence a metaphysical thesis. A realist accordingly takes it that a denial that the world is independent of discourse is a contradicting metaphysical thesis, amounting to an assertion of its existential dependence on the discourse. In the view of some, such as Rorty, this is indeed the implication. In the view of others, such as Dummett, Putnam and the argument here, this is not the implication; instead, the implication is that the independence of the world from discourse is *epistemological*.[7] What this means is as follows.[8]

The claim that the world-perception relation is epistemological says that discourse represents the world in a metaphysically innocent way. On a view such as Rorty's the very idea of 'representation' is suspect; how can we say that discourse is made true by the way things

---

[7]Cf. Richard Rorty, *Philosophy and the Mirror of Nature* (Princeton University Press 1979).

[8]Recurring to a debate that took place nearly a half-century and more ago might look old-fashioned. But inspection of that debate is peculiarly apt because it took place within a frame of assumptions, about to be bypassed though unresolved, in which the perennial philosophical problem of reality was cast in terms of an understanding of what a realist commitment entails that is luminously revealing. See R. Rorty, *Consequences of Pragmatism* (University of Minnesota Press 1982), 'Putnam and the Relativist Menace' *Journal of Philosophy* 90 (1993), 'Reply to Putnam.' In *Rorty and His Critics* ed. R. Brandon (Oxford University Press 2000); H. Putnam, *Representation and Reality* (MIT Press 1989), *Realism with a Human Face* (Harvard University Press 1990), *Words and Life* (Harvard University Press 1992); M. Dummett, *Truth and Other Enigmas* (Duckworth 1978), 'Realism' *Synthese* 52 (1982), *The Logical Basis of Metaphysics* (Harvard University Press 1991). Grayling, 'Metaphysically Innocent Representation' in *Truth, Meaning and Realism* 2007 is a first pass, much adjusted here, of the points at issue. The key cause of the difficulty then was the conception of truth in play.

are in the world if those things are not independent of our way of discoursing about them?[9] Rorty took Putnam to be an ally because Putnam argued that

> it makes no sense to think of the world as dividing itself up into "objects" (or "entities") independently of our use of language. It is *we* who divide up "the world" – that is, the events, states of affairs and physical, social etc., systems that we talk about – into "objects", "properties" and "relations", and we do this in a variety of ways.

In the terminology employed here, what both Rorty and Putnam are saying is that discourse projects ontology. A corollary of this, recognised by Putnam, is that different ontologies can be adopted for the same states of affairs, which means that apparently inconsistent pairs of statements can both be true in the sense of 'true in the way of speaking to which each belongs' (that is, paraconsistency in the sense employed here). Putnam called this 'conceptual relativity'.[10] But he repudiated Rorty's use of these thoughts to reject the putative dichotomy between the world and discourse of it, arguing that to do so depends upon making sense of the dichotomy, *metaphysically* understood, itself. For Putnam the idea of the 'independent existence' of actuals in the domain from discourse about them trades on notions of causal or logical independence that are not 'ordinary' ('in

---

[9]For medium-sized dry goods in the perceptual environment Wittgenstein's repudiation of an Augustinian view that learning begins with ostension is misplaced. The point that pointing and uttering a sound by itself does not distinguish whether it is the object itself, its colour, its use, its distance from the speaker, etc., and only understands which one of these is intended in the context of a convention, is right; but the learner acquires the convention by iterations of a form of Mill's Methods, and in doing so also picks up the import of the identifying and individuating descriptions supplied in the teaching given. The Augustine picture is not one of a bare utterance of 'Table!' together with ostension, but ostension together with iterated and context-variant such locutions as 'that thing there is a table', 'the colour of that table is brown', 'the dinner is on the table', etc.

[10]Hilary Putnam, *The Many Faces of Realism* (Open Court 1987).

the only way I can understand', he says); in the 'ordinary' sense of independence, the existence of objects and their properties allows a notion of representation made intelligible by 'conceptual relativism', the view that there are different descriptions – different ontologies – that can be adopted for them. Putnam accordingly argues that we can talk of referring to objects, but not in a metaphysically privileged way because there is a variety of ways of doing so, reprising his 'model theoretic' argument: 'we can think of our words and thoughts as having determinate reference to objects (when it is clear what sort of "objects" we are talking about and what vocabulary we are using); but there is no fixed sense of "reference" involved'.[11] He takes this to establish that there is no collapse of the notion of representation, and therefore no confinement within discourse such as is implied by a Rorty-type view; we therefore have a metaphysically innocent way of taking it that our discourse is *about* the word, that it *represents* the world, that our beliefs are *justified* by how the world is, because they recover the ordinary, 'humble' sense of such words as *represent, justified, thought, world*, quoting with approval Wittgenstein's remark that 'if the words "language", "experience", "world" have a use, it must be as humble a one as that of the words "table", "lamp", "door"'.

The problem with this recourse is its failure to see that whereas representation is metaphysically innocent, it is far from epistemologically innocent. More on this claim shortly. First, two immediate points are that to treat *true* 'humbly' is to treat it univocally, rejected in §§2 and 4 above, and by contrast to argue that there is 'no fixed sense of "reference" involved' is to fail to see the implication of the point that in all discourses reference works via descriptions, as is argued in §2, a direct corollary of the claim that discourses project

---

[11]Putnam, 'Models and Reality' in *Realism and Reason: Philosophical Papers*, Vol. 3 (Cambridge University Press 1983).

ontologies; though in this latter respect there is something right about the fact that acts of referring go via domain-specific descriptions in the relevant discourses, prompting Putnam's mistake that reference itself is therefore to be regarded equivocally, a mistake because referring is something discoursers do in all domains – it is the same speech-act in all of them – but how referring succeeds in attaching denoting expressions to their referents depends on how the referents are domain-dependently conceived (described); what varies is what secures the connection between the act and its target. In Putnam and Wittgenstein the move to deflating such concepts as 'representation', 'the world', 'experience', 'justification of beliefs', oddly accompanies retaining an inflated aspect of the concept of truth – its univocality – and in Putnam's case also a differently inflated concept of reference – its equivocality.

Moreover, Wittgenstein's move to closing down debate by relying on appeals to surface usage obscures the fact that discourses about the world and about tables are different in philosophically significant ways. If expressions such as 'world' and 'table' are on the same humble par, then how their senses are grasped works in the same way, which one sees cannot be right when one considers how their use is learned. One learns how to use 'table' (denoting an item of furniture) in acquiring a recognitional capacity for items that fall into the central extension of the term by their resemblance in form and function, or at least function, to samples one becomes acquainted with in learning the term.[12] To learn to talk of 'the world' requires considerably more factual knowledge and both linguistic and logical resources, and it does not involve a recognitional capacity anything like the kind

---

[12]It might be claimed here that Wittgenstein's conception of language games takes care of this point. In fact it is a concession to this point, and itself controverts his claim elsewhere that terms of putative philosophical significance should be deflated so that they share the humility of avowedly humble terms.

applied in talking about items of furniture. Whereas a generally close conformity of use in the linguistic community has to apply to 'table' for particular applications of the term to be successful, the associations of 'the world' admit of a much greater range, from planet Earth to the universe, from the aggregate of all things physical to social spheres and realities, determined by context. Understanding the context is part of grasping the sense of the term on an occasion of its use. 'Table' might be a humble word, but 'world' is not. This reprises the point against Austin and Wittgenstein in §2 that not all is in order with ordinary language.[13]

The idea that representation is not epistemologically innocent is key, because it fills out the account of the role played by the over-arching assumption that there is an ultimate reality, the assumption constitutive of metaphysical realism. In the debate involving Putnam and Dummett a univocal conception of substantive truth lay at the heart of their concerns. The latter defined 'semantic realism' as the thesis that the truth-conditions of statements can and often do outstrip speaker's competence to access them. By 'metaphysical realism' Putnam meant a set of theses about truth, these being 'that truth is a matter of Correspondence and that it exhibits Independence (of what humans do or could find out), Bivalence and Uniqueness (there cannot be more than one true or complete description of Reality)'.[14] He took 'Independence' to be 'radically non-epistemic' in line with Frege's sharp distinction between truth and grounds for truth, the point to which Dummett objected. It follows from Frege's claim that, as Putnam puts it, 'the world could be such that the theory

---

[13]Putnam, *Representation and Reality*, 107; Dummett *passim*.

[14]Putnam, 'Model Theory and the Factuality of Semantics' in A. George (ed.) *Reflections on Chomsky* (Blackwell 1989) 214.

we are most justified in accepting would not really be true ... rational acceptability is one thing, truth is another'.[15]

Certain interesting considerations arise from this. For the metaphysical realism presupposed in the background to natural science, the bivalence commitment is not only inessential but on the current face of it inapplicable, whereas the uniqueness commitment is essential. In a final physical theory the independence thesis would be existential; ultimate reality is not dependent for its existence or character on being cognised, though given that how it is cognised is dependent on facts about cognisers entails that the description of ultimate reality and description of cognition of it would coincide exactly – so the correspondence relation would be one of identity. In the discourse of perceptual experience the realistic attitude is different. It predicates bivalence, accepts non-uniqueness (the same phenomena admit of different and paraconsistent descriptions: *vide* the football match example in §3), and treats the concept of 'truth' (of grounds for predicating '__is true') as exhausted by defeasible rational assertibility (§4). This again marks the distinction between realism for a domain and metaphysical realism.

The most important point is the difference made by recognising that 'true' is equivocal across domains, for it is this that makes representation epistemologically guilty (to coin perforce a phrase). Consider the interconnected and overlapping forms which discourse-domain relations take: *perceiving*, which involves applying concepts and therefore (at least rudimentary, as in folk physics and psychology) theory; *referring* (picking out, individuating, identifying referents); *intending* (directing consciousness towards); *predicating of* (describing, qualifying, modifying); having beliefs about; *representing*, always under a description. 'Perceiving' in cases other than encounter

---

[15]In the offing again, Churchland, *Neurophilosophy* (MIT 1986).

with actuals in the domain of perceptual experience and science can be taken as covered by representation. In all cases domains consist in an ontology of referents, thus projections from the discourse; in all discourses the canons of enquiry specific to them nominate those that are actual; in some, chiefly the perceptual and scientific domains (including both natural and social science) the actuals are regarded realistically. In all these cases essential reference is made to what discoursers do in addressing the domain, where *essential* means what it says: reference to the discourse is ineliminable.

Once one understands that discourse ontologies are regarded realistically for purposes of conceptual housekeeping, and are discourse-dependent, the temptation to treat the concept of truth univocally is undermined. When we see that the predicate '__is true' is a placeholder for more informative predicates of evaluation individuated by the discourses in which they occur, we see that assimilating the semantic machinery of the discourse of perceptual experience to the semantic machinery of all other discourses removes the philosophical problems taken to arise from the reverse assimilation (the need e.g. for a Theory of Descriptions to defuse the existential commitments implicit in acts of referring).

Recall now the point that realism for the domain of perceptual and scientific discourses is a commitment to the hybridity of the relations between discourses and these domains: *internal* in the direction domain-to-discourse on broad content grounds, *external* in the direction discourse-to-domain on the grounds of the existential independence from discourse about them of the actuals in the domain. In asserting that reference to discourse is essential one is saying that the relation is *internal* in *both* directions; but in asserting that the direction discourse to domain is not *existential* – that the actuals do not causally or otherwise depend for their existence on discoursers – one is saying that the relation is purely epistemological.

But crucially this is asserted in light of the point that commitment to the existential independence of the actuals is strategic; that a realistic attitude to the domain is an undischargeable assumption for discourse about the domain to make sense. The one shift made is from treating this assumption as literally true to treating it as undischargeable if the discourse is to make sense.

Likewise the assumption of metaphysical realism – that there is an ultimate general reality – is the undischargeable assumption for making sense of assumptions of realism in domain-specific cases.

It covers the same ground as already covered to describe the assumptions in both cases as 'deferred', in effect as assumptions not up for challenge so long as they make sense of the discourses for which their sense-making assumption is required.

These points allow some tidying-up to be done. Consider again the terms of the debate in which Putnam's quasi-Wittgensteinian view was involved. This debate took for granted that, whether you were literally realist or literally non-realist about it, the touchstone of what would be real if it were real is the world of perceptual experience and – if you were also a realist about science – the science that explains it by reductive means. This assumption rendered problematic talk of any domain not consisting of spatio-temporal particulars and their microstructure; since 'truth' and 'reference' took their content from pretheoretical views about how they apply to the world of spatio-temporal particulars, they have to be deflated or redescribed in their application in other domains, thus generating the familiar menu of problems in question. Putnam recognised something about reference in recognising that 'it is *we* who divide up "the world"', choosing to equivocate the concept of reference itself; on the argument here the appropriate alternative is to recognise that it is the descriptive resources securing reference that differ by domain. To release truth from its bondage to the pretheoretically-assumed primacy of perceptual discourse and simultaneously taking seriously the ontology-projecting nature of natural language, is to pull the threads of the tapestry so that a different picture emerges, one in which the operation of realist commitments is properly understood, consistently with the internality of discourse-domain relations in both directions – the epistemological 'guilt' described.

In an earlier iteration of the perennial debate about the relation of discourse to domain – in practically all such iterations the domain in question was the spatio-temporal world – Charles Peirce said, 'But if it be asked whether some realities do not exist, which are entirely independent of thought; I would in turn ask, what is meant by such an expression and what can be meant by it. What idea can be attached to an idea of which there is no idea?'[16] His question has its answer here: we *do* have an idea of a reality (in fact, realities plural, one or more for each domain) existing independently of thought, in the form of an idea of the work done by realistic assumptions in their relevant domains, and – as the assumption that in turn gives these parochial assumptions their content – the idea of ultimate reality. In Peirce's question two separate matters are conflated, that of 'reality which is unknowable' and that of the question as to what an unknown reality could be (what it consists in). On the argument in the foregoing, the idea of an *intrinsically* unknowable reality is one (with the help of analogies) we only at best imagine we can conceive courtesy of negation on 'knowable' but is otherwise ungraspable – in this respect Peirce is right – while the fact that we have no candidate for what the unknown ultimate reality consists in is independent of the framing role that the *concept* of it plays, as the assumption which makes sense

---

[16]C. S. Peirce, *The Collected Papers of Charles Sanders Peirce*, eds. C. Hartshorne, P. Weiss (Vols. 1–6) and A. Burks (Vols. 7–8) (Harvard University Press 1931).

of realistic attitudes to domains in which they in their turn play a sense-making role.

The overall argument, therefore, is this: realism both for a domain and in the sense of a general commitment to there being an ultimate (final, irreducible) reality is an undischargeable assumption of thought and talk. The realist commitments in a domain are deferred – left to a separate argument about what it means – ultimately relying on the concept of metaphysical reality; this in turn is an *intrinsically* deferred concept, understanding of it exhausted by considerations of its role relative to domain-specific assumptions of realism. Coupling this with the view that discourses project ontologies via the grammatical roles of the terms occurring in them, that canons of enquiry for a domain selects what is to be treated as actual in it, and that all discourses are on a par in this respect, prompts accepting a revised understanding of truth, a descriptions theory of reference, an adjusted focus on modality, and acceptance of such consequences as that some, perhaps most, desired reductions (for the chief example, of perceptual discourse to the discourse of fundamental physics) can at best only be incomplete if possible at all.

This last point requires that we accept a patchwork view of 'the world' that our incompletely overlapping discourses present to us – better: that we inhabit a plurality of worlds, paraconsistently patched together in ways that are pragmatically justified for us at any point in our cognitive activity, but perennially renegotiated, adapted, extended and enriched as the canons of enquiry in each do the same thing internally, thus requiring external adaptations to its relations with discourses neighbouring it. That this is in fact so is an empirical datum. Such relations motivate evaluating a given domain of discourse in the light of other domains; for example, considerations in the domains of perceptual experience and science offer strong reasons for thinking that whereas the domain of religious discourse has sociological, psychological and historical interest, it has no reciprocal value for what is accorded facticity in the evaluating domains. Driving enquiry internally in a domain and adjusting our conception of how domains relate is an overarching assumption: that there can be a final unifying account of how everything is. That assumption is strategic, and by the argument here indispensable, not just to understanding the point of enquiry but to making sense of what we think and say as we inhabit the worlds of our discourses.

The bottom line is that the question about reality which is not only right but the only possible question is not 'What is ultimately real?' but 'What work does the concept of "reality" do?' And the answer is, the concept of reality stands off to the side in our discourses, in the corner of the conceptual eye, when we refer, describe, and make truth-claims (when we assert); and when we turn to the concept itself as it applies in that domain in determining questions of what is *actual* within it, we find that off to the side again – a further side – is the concept of *ultimate* reality as giving borrowed content to the idea of 'what exists, what is real' in the domain, either in applying or denying this status; and when we turn to the concept of ultimate reality itself, in turn yet again, we find that it applies to nothing but the work it does, in providing anchorage for the epistemic task of classifying as 'actual' those referents in a given domain that, by the canons of enquiry applicable to it, comprise the target subset of that domain's total ontology of referents. Whereas the question of what is 'real' in any domain is deferrable to this final resource, the question of 'ultimate reality' itself is *intrinsically* deferrable, explicable only in terms of the work it does as the deferred sense-maker for realist commitments within particular domains.

'Ultimate reality', in short, is not a thing but a concept; the assumption that there is such a thing is undischargeable, the meaning of the phrase is wholly given by its use, the Cretan Paradox-like ascription of ultimate reality to 'ultimate reality' the source of many philosophical perplexities. At the same time, to say this is not to say that the chair on which I sit and the desk at which I write are any less real than they have ever been. The reals are the actuals determined by the canons of enquiry of a given domain, and practice enters into the justification of their being identified as such. What this thesis states, therefore – and modestly enough – is that the claim that 'x is real' is always implicitly 'x is real in the domain of (the given) discourse', reference to a given discourse being ineliminable in all cases.

References and Select Bibliography

Austen, J. L. *Sense and Sensibilia*, ed., G. J. Warnock (Oxford University Press 1962).

Austen, J. L. *Philosophical Papers*, 3rd edn., eds. J. O. Urmson and G. J. Warnock (Oxford University Press 1979).

Ayer, A. J. *The Problem of Knowledge* (Pelican Books 1956).

Ayer, A. J. *Logical Positivism* (Free Press 1966).

Ayer, A. J. *The Central Questions of Philosophy* (Weidenfeld 1973).

Bach, E. 'Natural Language Metaphysics'. In *Logic, Methodology and Philosophy of Science VII*, eds. R. B. Marcus, G. J. W. Dorn, and P. Weingartner (Studies in Logic and the Foundations of Mathematics 114) (Elsevier 1986).

Berkeley, G. *A Treatise Concerning the Principles of Human Knowledge* (Dublin 1710).

Berkeley, G. *A Three Dialogues Between Hylas and Philonous* (Dublin 1713).

Blackburn, P., Hasle, P. and Øhrstrøm, P. (eds.), *Logic and Philosophy of Time* (Aalborg University Press 2019).

Blackburn, S. 'History of the Philosophy of Language'. In T. Honderich (ed.) *The Oxford Companion to Philosophy* (Oxford University Press 1995).

Block, N. 'Advertisement for a Semantics for Psychology'. In P. French, T. Uehling and H. Wettstein (eds.) *Midwest Studies in Philosophy*, vol. 10 (1986) 615–678.

Burge, T. 'Philosophy of Language and Mind' *Philosophical Review* 101 (1992).

Burge, T. *Truth, Thought and Reason* (Oxford University Press 2005).

Burge, T. *Origins of Objectivity* (Oxford University Press 2010).

Callender, C. *The Oxford Handbook of the Philosophy of Time* (Oxford University Press 2013).

Carnap, R. 'Empiricism, Semantics, and Ontology', *Revue Internationale de Philosophie* 4(11) (1950); reprinted in Carnap, *Meaning and Necessity: A Study in Semantics and Modal Logic*, 2nd edn. (University of Chicago Press 1956).

Carnap, R. *Meaning and Necessity: A Study in Semantics and Modal Logic*, 2nd edn. (University of Chicago Press 1956).

Carnap, R. 'On the Character of Philosophic Problems' trans. W. M. Malisoff (Carnap Project: Benson No. 1934-1).

Carnap, R. *The Logical Structure of the World* (Open Court 2003).

Cartwright, N. *How the Laws of Physics Lie* (Oxford University Press 1983).

Churchland, P. 'The Ontological Status of Observables'. In P. M. Churchland and C. A. Hooker (eds.) *Images of Science* (Chicago University Press 1985).

Churchland, P. *Neurophilosophy: Toward a Unified Science of the Mind-Brain* (MIT 1986).

Churchland, P. *The Dappled World: A Study of the Boundaries of Science* (Cambridge University Press 1999).

Clarke, S. *The Leibniz-Clarke Correspondence*, ed. H. G. Alexander (Manchester University Press 1956).

Collingwood, R. G. *Speculum Mentis* (Oxford University Press 1924).

Collins, W. A. 'Types, Rigidity and A Posteriori Necessity' *Midwest Studies* XII (1988).

Comrie, B. *Tense* (Cambridge University Press 1985).

Crane, T. 'All the Difference in the World' *Philosophical Quarterly* 41 (1991).

Crane, T. (ed.) *The Contents of Experience* (Cambridge University Press 1992).

Crane, T. *The Objects of Thought* (Oxford University Press 2013).

Cubitt, T. S. et al. 'The Undecidability of the Spectral Gap' *Forum of Mathematics, Pi* 10 (2022), 2015.

Curado, M. and Gouveia, S. S. (eds.), *Perception, Cognition and Aesthetics* (Routledge/Taylor & Francis Group 2019).

Davidson, D. 'Reality Without Reference', 'A Coherence Theory of Truth and Knowledge'. In E. Lepore (ed.) *Truth and Interpretation* (Blackwell 1986).

Davidson, D. 'The Folly of Trying to Define Truth' *Journal of Philosophy* Vol. XCIII (1996).

Davidson, D. *Enquiries into Truth and Interpretation* (Oxford University Press 2001).

Davidson, D. *Truth and Predication* (Belknap Press 2005).

Davidson, D. *Truth, Language and History* (Oxford University Press 2005).

Davidson, D. 'Truth and Indefinability'. In *Truth, Meaning and Realism* (Continuum 2007).

Davidson, D. *The Structure of Truth* (Oxford University Press 2020).

Dummett, M. *Frege: Philosophy of Language* (Duckworth 1973).

Dummett, M. *Truth and Other Enigmas* (Duckworth 1978).

Dummett, M. *The Interpretation of Frege's Philosophy* (Harvard University Press 1981).

Dummett, M. 'Realism' *Synthese* 52 (1982): 55–112.

Dummett, M. *The Logical Basis of Metaphysics* (Harvard University Press 1991).

Dummett, M. *Philosophy of Language* (Polity 2013).

Evans, G. (ed. McDowell, J.) *The Varieties of Refence* (Oxford University Press 1982).

Evans, G. (ed. McDowell, J.) *Collected Papers* (Oxford University Press 1985).

Evans, G. and McDowell, J. (eds.) *Truth and Meaning* (Oxford University Press 1976).

Feyerabend, P. *Against Method* (New Left Books 1975).

Field, H. 'Logic, Meaning and Conceptual Role' *Journal of Philosophy* 74 (1977).

Fine, A. 'The Natural Ontological Attitude'. In J. Kourany, *Scientific Knowledge*, 2nd edn. (Cengage Learning 1997). See also his 'And Not Anti-Realism Either' *ibid.*

Fine, A. *The Shaky Game: Einstein, Reaism and the Quantum Theory* (University of Chicago Press 2009).

Fine, K. *Modality and Tense* (Oxford University Press 2005).

Fine, K. 'Naive Metaphysics', *Philosophical Issues* 27(1) (2017).

Fodor, J. 'Special Sciences, or the Disunity of Science' *Synthese* 28 (1974).

Fodor, J. *The Language of Thought* (Harvard University Press 1975).

Foster, D. Z. 'Will String Theory Finally Be Put to the Experimental Test?' *Scientific American*, March 2020.

Frege, G. 'Über Sinn und Bedeutung'. In *Zeitschrift für Philosophie und philosophische Kritik* 100 (1892), translated as 'On Sense and Reference' by M. Black in Geach and Black (eds. and trans.), 1980.

Frege, G. *Collected Papers on Mathematics, Logic, and Philosophy*, ed. McGuinness B. (Blackwell 1984).

Galison, P. and Stump D. J. (eds.) *The Disunity of the Sciences: Boundaries, Contexts, and Power* (Stanford University Press 1996).

Goodman, N. *Ways of Worldmaking* (Hacket 1978).

Gouveia, S. S. and Northoff, G. 'A Neurophilosophical Approach to Perception'. In D. Shottenkirk, M. Curado and S. S. Gouveia (eds.) *Perception, Cognition and Aesthetics* (Routledge 2019) 41–63.

Grayling, A. C. *The Refutation of Scepticism* (Duckworth 1976).

Grayling, A. C. 'Internal Structure and Essence' *Analysis* 42 (1982).

Grayling, A. C. *An Introduction to Philosophical Logic*, 3rd edn. (Blackwell 1997).

Grayling, A. C. 'Russell, Experience and the Roots of Science'. In N. Griffin (ed.) *The Cambridge Companion to Bertrand Russell* (Cambridge University Press 2003).

Grayling, A. C. *Truth, Meaning and Realism* (Continuum 2007).

Grayling, A. C. *The Frontiers of Knowledge* (Viking 2021).

Grayling, A. C. with Wuppuluri, S. *Metaphors and Analogies in Sciences and Humanities* (Synthese Library Vol. 453) (Springer 2022).

Grice, P. *Studies in the Ways of Words* (Harvard University Press 1967).

Grice, P. 'Utterer's Meaning and Intentions' *The Philosophical Review* 78 (1969).

Hacker, P. M. S. 'Events, Ontology, and Grammar,' *Philosophy* 57 (1982).

Hale, B. *Abstract Objects* (Blackwell 1987).

Hale, B. with Wright, C. *A Companion to the Philosophy of Language* (Blackwell 1999).

Hale, B. *Necessary Beings* (Oxford University Press 2013).

Harman, G. with Davidson, D. (eds.) *Semantics of Natural Language* (Reidel 1972).

Harman, G. with Davidson, D. (eds.) *Scepticism and the Definition of Knowledge* (Garland 1990).

Harman, G. with Davidson, D. (eds.) *Reasoning, Meaning and Mind* (Oxford University Press 1999).

Harrison, B. *Form and Content* (Blackwell 1973).

Harrison, B. (with Hanna, P.) *Word and World* (Cambridge University Press 2003).

Hauser, M., Chomsky, N. and Fitch, W. T. 'The Faculty of Language: What Is It, Who Has It, and How Did It Evolve' *Science* 298 (2002): 1569–79.

Hempel, C. *Aspects of Scientific Explanation* (Free Press 1965).

Hooker, C. A. *Toward a General Theory of Reduction* (Dialogue 20) (Cambridge University Press 1981).

Huemer, M. and Kovitz, B. 'Causation as Simultaneous and Continuous' *Philosophical Quarterly* 53 (2003).

Hume, D. *A Treatise of Human Nature* (London 1739–40).

Hurford, J. R. 'Nativist and Functional Explanations in Language Acquisition'. In I. M. Roca (ed.) *Logical Issues in Language Acquisition* (Reidel 1995).

Jammer, M. *The Philosophy of Quantum Mechanics* (Wiley 1974).

Jones, R. H. *Analysis & the Fullness of Reality: An Introduction to Reductionism & Emergence* (Jackson Square Books 2013).

Kahneman, D. *Thinking Fast and Slow* (Viking 2011).

Kamp, H. 'The Paradox of the Heap' (1981). In U. Münnich (ed.) *Aspects of Philosophical Logic* (Cambridge University Press 1996).

Kant, I. *Critique of Pure Reason*. In P. Guyer and A. Wood (eds.) *The Cambridge Edition of the Works of Immanuel Kant* (Cambridge University Press 1992–).

Kim, J. *Explanatory Realism, Causal Realism, and Explanatory Exclusion* (Midwest Studies 12) (Elsevier 1988).

Kretzmann, N., Kenny, A. and Pinborg, J. (eds.) *The Cambridge History of Later Medieval Philosophy* (Cambridge University Press 1982).

Kripke, S. *Naming and Necessity* (Harvard University Press 1980).

Lance, M. and O'Leary-Hawthorne, J. *The Grammar of Meaning* (Cambridge University Press 1997).

LePore, E. and Smith, B. C. (eds.) *The Oxford Handbook of Philosophy of Language* (Oxford University Press 2006).

Lewis, D. *Philosophical Papers, Vols. I & II* (Oxford University Press 1983, 1986).

Locke, J. *An Essay Concerning Human Understanding* (1689).

Loss, R. 'Open Future, Supervaluationism and the Growing-Block Theory: A Stage-Theoretical Account' *Synthese* 199 (2021).

Maloney, Thomas S. *Roger Bacon on Signs*: Translated with an Introduction and Notes. *Mediaeval Sources in Translation* (Pontifical Institute of Mediaeval Studies, 2013).

McDowell, J. *Mind and World* (Harvard University Press 1994).

McDowell, J. 'The Content of Perceptual Experience' *Philosophical Quarterly* 44 (1994).

McDowell, J. *Having the World in View* (Harvard University Press 2009).

McGinn, C. *The Subjective View* (Oxford University Press 1983).

McGinn, C. 'Can We Solve the Mind-Body Problem' *Mind* 98 (1989).

McTaggart, J. M. E. 'The Unreality of Time', *Mind* 17 (1908): 457–73; reprinted in McTaggart, *The Nature of Existence*, Vol. 2 (Cambridge University Press 1927).

Nagel, E. *The Structure of Science* (Routledge 1961).

Nagel, T. *The View from Nowhere* (Oxford University Press 1986).

Neurath, O. 'Radical Physicalism and the "Real World"'. In R. S. Cohen and M. Neurath (eds.) *Philosophical Papers 1913–1946* (Reidel 1983).

Oliver, A. and Smiley, T. *Plural Logic* (Oxford University Press 2013).

Ottinger, H. C. 'Elementary Particles with Zero Spin Must Be Massless' *ArXiv Physics* (arXiv:2401.17344) January 2024.

Pears, D. 'Is Existence a Predicate?' In P. Strawson (ed.) *Philosophical Logic*: *Oxford Readings in Philosophy* (Oxford University Press 1967).

Pears, D. *Questions in the Philosophy of Mind* (Barnes and Noble 1975).

Peirce, C. S. *The Collected Papers of Charles Sanders Peirce*, eds. C. Hartshorne, P. Weiss (Vols. 1–6) and A. Burks (Vols. 7–8, Harvard University Press 1931).

Plato. *Parmenides* (Perseus Digital Library Tufts University).

Platts, M. *Ways of Meaning*, 2nd edn. (MIT Press 1997).

Popper, K. *Conjectures and Refutations* (Basic Books 1962).

Popper, K. *The Logic of Scientific Discovery* (Routledge 2002).

Potochnik, A. *Idealization and the Aims of Science* (University of Chicago Press 2017).

Price, H. 'Truth and the Nature of Assertion' *Mind* 86(382) (1987).

Price, H. *Facts and the Function of Truth* (Oxford University Press 1988).

Putnam, H. *Philosophy of Logic* (Harper & Row 1971).

Putnam, H. *Mind, Language and Reality* (Cambridge University Press 1975).

Putnam, H. 'Models and Reality'. In *Realism and Reason: Philosophical Papers, Vol. 3* (Cambridge University Press 1983).

Putnam, H. *The Many Faces of Realism* (Open Court 1987).

Putnam, H. 'Model Theory and the Factuality of Semantics'. In A. George (ed.) *Reflections on Chomsky* (Blackwell 1989).

Putnam, H. *Representation and Reality* (MIT Press 1989).

Putnam, H. *Realism with a Human Face* (Harvard University Press 1990).

Putnam, H. *Words and Life* (Harvard University Press 1992).

Quine, W. V. 'On What There Is' *The Review of Metaphysics* 2(1) (1948); reprinted in Quine, *From a Logical Point of View* (Harper 1953).

Quine, W. V. *Word and Object* (MIT 1960).

Quine, W. V. *Ontological Relativity and Other Essays* (Columbia University Press 1969).

Quine, W. V. *The Ways of Paradox* (Harvard University Press 1976).

Ramsey F. P. 'Facts and Propositions' (1927); reprinted in *F.P. Ramsey: Philosophical Papers*, ed. D. H. Mellor (Cambridge University Press 1990).

Reichenbach, H. *Elements of Symbolic Logic* (Dover Publications 1947).

Rorty, R. *Philosophy and the Mirror of Nature* (Princeton University Press 1979).

Rorty, R. *Consequences of Pragmatism* (University of Minnesota Press 1982).

Rorty, R. 'Putnam and the Relativist Menace' *Journal of Philosophy* 90 (1993).

Rorty, R. 'Reply to Putnam'. In R. Brandon (ed.) *Rorty and His Critics* (Oxford University Press 2000).

Rowbottom, D. P. 'The Instrumentalist's New Clothes' *Philosophy of Science* 78(5) (2011).

Russell, B. 'On Denoting' *Mind* 14(56) (1905): 469–493.

Ryle, G. 'Systematically Misleading Expressions' *Proceedings of the Aristotelian Society* 32 (1932).

Ryle, G. *Dilemmas* (Cambridge University Press 1960).

Schaffner, K. F. 'Approaches to Reduction' *Philosophy of Science* 34 (1967).

Schaffner, K. F. *Discovery and Explanation in Biology and Medicine* (Chicago University Press 1993).

Searle, J. *Speech Acts: An Essay in the Philosophy of Language* (Cambridge University Press 1969).

Sellars, W. *Science, Perception and Reality* (Routledge 1963).

Sellars, W. *Science and Metaphysics* (Ridgeview 1969).

Sellars, W. *Naturalism and Ontology* (Ridgeview 1979).

Sellars, W. *The Metaphysics of Epistemology*, ed. P. Amaral (Ridgeview 1989).

Sellars, W. *Empiricism and the Philosophy of Mind* (Harvard University Press 1997).

Stainton, R. J. *Philosophical Perspectives on Language* (Broadview Press 1996).

Strawson, P. F. *Individuals* (Methuen 1959).

Strawson, P. F. *The Bounds of Sense* (Methuen 1966).

Strawson, P. F. *Logico-Linguistic Papers* (Methuen 1971).

Strawson, P. F. 'Truth'. In *Logico-Linguistic Papers* (Methuen 1971).

Strawson, P. F. 'Identifying Reference and Truth-Values' *Theoria* 30 (1964): 96–118; reprinted in *Logico-linguistic Papers* (Methuen 1971).

Szabo, Z. 'Major Parts of Speech'. *Erkenntnis* 80 (2015).

Szabo, Z. 'An Object-Based Truthmaker Theory for Modals' *Philosophical Issues* 28(1) (2018).

Tarski, A. 'The Concept of Truth in Formalized Languages'. In J. H. Woodger, *Logic, Semantics, Metamathematics* (Oxford University Press 1956) 152–278, and 'The Semantic Conception of Truth'. In H. Feigl and W. Sellars, *Readings in Philosophical Analysis* (Appleton-Century-Crofts 1949).

Torza, A. 'Natural Language and Its Ontology'. In A. Goldman and B. McLaughlin (eds.) *Metaphysics and Cognitive Science* (Oxford University Press 2019).

Turri, J. *Knowledge and the Norm of Assertion* (Open Book 2016).

van Fraasen, B. *The Scientific Image* (Clarendon Press 1980).

van Fraasen, B. *Scientific Representation* (Oxford University Press 2010).

Weissenstein, A. et al. 'Alice in Wonderland Syndrome' *Journal of Pediatric Neurosciences* 9(3) (2014).

Wigner, E. 'The Unreasonable Effectiveness of Mathematics in the Natural Sciences' *Communications on Pure and Applied Mathematics* 13(91) (1960).

Williams, B. *Truth and Truthfulness* (Princeton University Press 2004).

Wittgenstein, L. *Philosophical Investigations*, G. E. M. Anscombe and R. Rhees (eds.), G. E. M. Anscombe (trans.) (Blackwell 1953).

Wittgenstein, L. *On Certainty*, G. E. M. Anscombe and G. H. von Wright (eds.), G. E. M. Anscombe and D. Paul (trans.) (Blackwell 1969).

Wittgenstein, L. *Tractatus Logico-Philosophicus*, trans. D. Pears and B. McGuiness, 2nd edn. (Routledge, 2001).

Wright, C. *Realism, Meaning and Truth* (Blackwell 1986).

Wright, C. 'Realism, Antirealism, Irrealism, Quasi-Realism'. In P. A. French et al., *Midwest Studies in Philosophy XII: Realism and Antirealism* (University of Minnesota Press 1988).

Wright, C. *Truth and Objectivity* (Harvard University Press 1993).

Wright, C. *Saving the Differences* (Harvard University Press 2003).

References in the Preface to Books by the Author Not Cited in the Main Bibliography

Philosophy:

The Refutation of Scepticism (Duckworth 1975); *Berkeley: The Central Arguments* (Duckworth 1976); *Wittgenstein* (Oxford University Press 1988); (as editor) *Philosophy I: A Guide Through the Subject* (Oxford University Press 1995); (as editor) *Philosophy II: Further Through the Subject* (Oxford University Press 1998); *Russell* (Oxford University Press 1996); (as editor with Goulder, N. and Pyle, A.) *The Continuum Encyclopaedia of British Philosophy* (Thoemmes Continuum, 4 vols., 2006); *Descartes* (Simon and Schuster 2006); *Scepticism and the Possibility of Knowledge* (Continuum 2008); (as editor with Copson, A.) *The Wiley Handbook of Humanism* (Wiley-Blackwell 2015); *The History of Philosophy* (Viking 2019); *Philosophy and Life* (Viking 2023).

History of Ideas:

Towards the Light (Bloomsbury 2011); *The Age of Genius* (Bloomsbury 2016); *The Frontiers of Knowledge* (Viking 2021).

Politics:

Democracy and Its Crisis (Oneworld 2017); *The Good State* (Oneworld 2020); *For the Good of the World* (Oneworld 2022); *Who Owns the Moon* (Oneworld 2024); *Discriminations* (Oneworld 2025); *For the People* (Oneworld 2025).

Index

absolute logical necessity, notion 126
abstract entities 14, 15
acceptability
    assertion solicitation, relationship
        65–6
    desiderata 65, 66
acceptance, reliability (commitment)
    74–5
accepted assertion, fact (metaterm) 72
action, moral quality 27–8
activity, modalities 12
actuality
    achievement 143
    contrast, example 141
    proposition, formulation 123
actuals
    classification, epistemic task
        (anchorage) 160
    concept, collapse 17
    notions 142
    realism 149–50
adequacy, relationship 65–6
Against Method (Feyerabend) 9 n.7
agniology, acceptance 109–10
'All the Difference in the World'
    (Crane) 94 n.5
analogy
    role 77
    simile, contrast 81–2
    usage 2

Anglophone philosophy 109–10
anti-realist point 139–40
a priori principles 134
A-properties, relations 43
A-property-predicating statement
    possession, requirement 43
arguments, pertinence (philosophical
    tradition) 6
Aristotelian intuition, examination 21
Aristotle
    birth/study 25
    common sense postulation 32–3
    laws of thought 126
    reference 22
    sea-battle 44
artificial kind sortals,
    determinateness 96
A-series concepts 42
    B-series concepts, connection 45
    dependence 47
    inconsistency, disappearance 42–3
A-series properties, predication 45
A-series requirements 43–4
Aspects of Scientific Explanation
    (Hempel) 102 n.12
assertibility-in-a-domain, impact
    68–9
assertibillity, examples 64
assertions
    aspiration 75

class 73
  defeasibility 75
  expression, epistemic attitude
    (relationship) 74
  fact-stating discourse, equivalence
    71–2
  long iterations 27
  metaphorical assertions 78
  mimicry 73
  perlocutionary aim 68–9
  perlocutionary forces 65
  precisification 53–4
  pretended assertion 75–6
  speech-act 60
  theory, formulation 60
  truth, interdependence 73
  truth, relationship 59
  truth-values 28
assertoric mode 14
assertoric practice 65–6
astronomical beliefs, hypothetical
    23–4
Augustinian view, Wittgenstein
    repudiation 151 n.9
Austen, Jane 19

baptised entity 22
basal conceptual scheme 33
basal ontology 1, 36
B-dependent A-series concepts 44
being, propositions (distinction) 124
beliefs, justification 153
benzene, carbon atom ring 130–1
Bergsonian duration 41
Berkeley, George (cognitive
    neuropsychology alignment) 33
Berkeley: The Central Arguments
    (Grayling) 33 n.3, 146 n.5
biconditional statements, logical
    form 127
bivalence 154–5
  commitment 155

Block perspective 48
Block theory 41
Block Universe conception 42
Block Universe view 41
blurred-boundary subdiscourses 17
body-talk, ontologies (projection) 38
border/borderlessness, problem
    51–2
boundary, drawing 99–100
brain
    microstructure, examination 38
    structures, activation 80
brain-mind, usage 33
broad meaning, narrow meaning
    (distinction) 93
Bronze Age Collapse 48
B-series concepts 42
    A-series concepts, connection 45
    A-series concepts, dependence 47
    truth-condition work 42–3
B-series terms, connection 43
Burns, Robbie (simile, usage) 82

Caesium-133, oscillation 40 n.6
'canons of enquiry' 115–16
causal dynamics 47
causal nexuses, statements 47
causal theory 29
    predication 67
causes/effects, temporal relations
    46–7
ceteris paribus clause 122
Churchland, Patricia 102
Cicero 62
city context, distance (description) 47
claim, *prima facie* appearance 134
classical horizon 36–7
closure problem 114
cognisers
    claim 138
    facts, dependence 155
cognitive architecture 85–6

cognitive assimilation,
    power (metaphorical
    exploitation) 79
cognitive capacity 34–5
    levels, analogy 139
cognitive endowments 89
cognitive modalities, role 32
cognitive neuropsychology,
    alignments 33
cognitive neuroscience, observations
    3–4
cognitive role, importance
    (underplaying) 78
*Collected Papers of Charles Sanders
    Peirce, The* (Peirce) 158 n.16
*Collected Papers on Mathematics,
    Logic, and Philosophy*
    (McGuinness) 53 n.16
combustible materials, proximity 50
commonalities, description 14
common sense, Aristotelian
    postulation 32–3
communicability 89
communication
    brevity/facility 69
    vague expressions, utility 54–5
communicative ends, achievement 49
communicative intention/context,
    impact 44
communicative success
    achievement 56
    role 70
communicative utility,
    undermining 55
compass points, fashion 49–50
complex statement, uttering 24
composition, fallacy 97
conceivability 139
    constraint 131
    meaning 129–30
    modal concept 127–8

modal notion 120
    requirement 119–20
concept
    content, addition 95–6
    grasping 94–5
conceptions, usage 94, 96
'Concept of Truth in Formalized
    Languages, The' (Tarski) 69 n.8
'Concept-Reference and Natural
    Kinds' (Grayling) 93 n.3
conceptual commitments 74
conceptual content, cross-application
    partial aspect 85
    transitive power 84
conceptual insight, expression 83–4
conceptual metaphor theory 79
conceptual relativity 151–2
conceptual schemes 31
    ad hoc nature 33–4, 37, 46, 49
    basal ontology 36
    discourse-presupposition 86
    embodiment 29
    ontology 97
    patchwork nature,
        demonstration 39
    proposition 123
    structural elements 34
    structural elements, multiple/
        non-overlapping nature 37
conceptual weight, transfer 63
concrete particulars, domain 15
concrete spatio-temporal entities,
    realm 25
conditional epistemic necessity 122
conditionality, universalisation 127
conditional necessity, statement 127
conditional Principle of Sufficient
    Reason 125
conjunctions
    chains 60
    development 12

connections, matrix 85–6
consciousness 133
    direction 155
Consequences of Pragmatism (Rorty)
        150 n.8
constellation, referents
        (equivalence) 24
constrained conformities 97
constructability, discussion 69
content, cross-application 85
content-narrow content
        distinction 38
context-dependent fuller account,
        placeholder (role) 26
context-individuating movement,
        necessity 21
contingency (contingencies) 122–3
    specification 130
contingent matters, assertions 60
Copernican view, acceptance 113
copula
    logical category 81
    logical character, equivalence 80
corrective supplement 24
correctness, concept
        (consideration) 57
correspondence 154–5
    theory 66–7
cosmology, microstructure 113
counterfactuals 127
cultures, glosses 33

Dappled World, The: A Study of
        the Boundaries of Science
        (Cartwright) 101 n.11
data
    harvesting 112, 115–16
    storage 116
Davidson, Donald 59
dead-and-alive cat analogy
        (Schrodinger) 82

declarative sentences, non-trivial
        spatio-temporally indexed
        utterances 60
decoherence 2 n.1
defeasibility, epistemic fact 64
deference, concept 145
deferral 137
    concept 135
    sense, explication 91
deferred commitment 145–6
definitional stipulations 51
deflationary claim, resistance 69
deflationism, characterisation 59
deity
    attitudes/commands,
        discourse 145
    notion, independent
        implausibility 147
demon possession, psychiatry usage
        (disappearance) 141
De Morgan's Theorem 126
denotatum 147
deoxyribonucleic acid (DNA),
        purification 117
Descartes, Rene 109, 130
    imaging connotation 130–1
descriptions
    application 25
    cluster 24–5
    disjunction, minimum 24
    usage 152–3
descriptive knowledge, reference
        (relationship) 22
desuetude 28
determinate conditions, absence
        51–2
determiners, development 12
dilemma, resolution 39
Dilemmas (Ryle) 125 n.11
direct causal history 22
disanalogies 83–4

disbelief, tones 60
discourse
  application, incommensurable
    quality 37–8
  assimilation 18
  commensuraiblity 38
  conceptual schemes,
    embodiment 29
  concept, usage 17
  domain 65
  domains, grammar 15
  grammar (ontology) 14–15
  language, meanings (publicity/
    stability) 76
  ordinary discourse,
    imprecisions 50
  reducing discourse 102
  reduction 86
  total ontology 140
  understanding 98–9
discourse (ontology)
  assimilation, attempt 38–9
  organisation 8–9
  privileging 19–20
  privileging, question 7
  projection 16, 152–3
  understanding 156
discourse-domain relations 155–6
discourse-presupposition 86
discourse-relative 25
discourse-relative predicates 69
discourse-relativity 26, 76
discoursers
  cognitive activities 139–40
  cognitive capacities 139–40
  cognitive powers 138
  direction 139
  existence 156–7
discourse to domain (direction) 8
Discovery and Explanation in
  Biology and Medicine
  (Schaffner) 107 n.20

discovery, defining 118–19
disjunctions, chains 60
dispositional properties,
  accounts 127
disquotationalism 59
distortion, introduction
  (avoidance) 113
disvalued propositions 66
doctrine of real essences, revival 90
domain
  commitments 135
  constitution 36–7
  direction 139
  disputes 145
  enquiry, canons 135
  intelligibility/functioning 15
  ontology 16, 139–40, 143
  picture 115
  realism 137–8
  realism, commitment 135
  realistic attitudes 159
  reduction, conceptual safety 113
  reference, differences 27
  understanding 79
domain to discourse (direction) 8
Donnellan-type case 24
double commitment, realism
  denotation 137
durations, incomplete/complete
  status (denotation) 43

electromagnetic spectrum, ranges
  (existence) 133
elementary particles, concepts
  (deferrability) 147–8
'Elementary Particles with Zero Spin
  Must Be Massless' (Ottinger)
  148 n.6
Elements of Symbolic Logic
  (Reichenbach) 44 n.11
empirical adequacy 5
empirical datum 159

empirically-accessible environment 72
empirical results, neurophilosophy
    invocation 32
'Empiricism, Semantics, and
    Ontology' (Carnap) 16 n.4
empty-full 126
enquiry 109
    airms 129–30
    canons, impact 128
    'canons of enquiry' 115–16
    commitment 129
    content, addition 95–6
    direction 106
    driving 160
    methodology 131
    processes 87
    process, framing 99
    psychological considerations 114
    psychology 130–1
    realist assumptions, strategic
        role 98–9
    resource 78
    social science enquiry 117
entanglement 2
    metaphor 118–19
entropy, concept 41–2
epicycles, Hipparchian concept
    (usage) 113
epidemiology, concern 117
epistemic agency, idea 134
epistemic attitude (expression),
    assertion (relationship) 74
epistemic forms, reductionism
    (relationship) 104
epistemic modality
    account 121–2
    attention 126–7
epistemic possibility 127–8
epistemic reduction 104–5
epistemic situation 128–9
epistemic terms 68
epistemic utility 59

epistemological role 149
epistemological scepticism, lessons 37
epistemology
    difference, absence 86
    human being achievement 117
error, risk 109
*Essay Concerning Human
    Understanding, An* (Locke)
    40 n.7
essentialism, commitment
    (absence) 25
eternal sentences, existence 62 n.4
Euclidean plane angle, trisection
    124 n.11, 128 n.12, 131
evaluation
    criteria 67–8
    function, predicates 26
    informative predicates 156
event time 44
evolutionary history, length
    48 n.14
existents, progressive
    accumulation 41
experience
    carving up 35–6
    organisation 34
    term, use 152
*Explanatory Realism, Causal Realism,
    and Explanatory Exclusion*
    (Kim) 102 n.14
explanatory terminus 125
explanatory value, incomplete
    reductions (idea) 18
'Explicit Speaker Theory' (Grayling)
    29 n.9
expressions, use (assimilation) 100
expressivist reading 72–3
external domain 156–7
extra-theoretical criteria 114

façon de parler 61, 128, 141
fact, duality 66–7

'Facts and Propositions' (Ramsey)
        60 n.2
fact-stating
    dependence 72
    discourse, assertion (equivalence)
        71–2
'Faculty of Language: What Is It,
        Who Has It, and How Did It
        Evolve' (Hauser/Chomsky/
        Fitch) 13 n.2
falsehoods
    presence 103
    purveying 75–6
falsification, introduction
        (avoidance) 113
fast thinking (Kahneman) 114
fearing (intentional phenomena)
        80–1
fictional realms 14, 15
'figures of speech' 78
Fine, Arthur (Natural Ontological
        Attitude invocation) 5–6
finite cognitive powers, inference
        128–9
finite epistemic capacities,
        transcendence 94
fire, term (application) 50
focal cases, identification (ability)
        51–2
'Folly of Trying to Define Truth,
        The' (Davidson) 27 n.8
formal languages, semantics
        (discussion) 69
formal system, axioms/derivation
        rules (usage) 122
Form and Content (Harrison) 49 n.15
forward history, bifurcation 83
framework-providing role 149
Fregean objectivity, necessity
        (absence) 97
Frisen, Jonas 116

From a Logical Point of View (Quine)
        16 n.4
Frontiers of Knowledge, The
        (Grayling) 112 n.3
future-tensed discourse, mastery
        (representation) 46
future-tensed statements,
        truth-value 44

general terms, denotata 58
generic expressions 34
generic term 69–70
grammar
    ontologies, implicitness 89
    surface forms 20
grammatical ontology 89
gravitation, Newtonian theories
        113 n.5
Gricean constraints 97
groupings, natural kinds
        (comparison) 89
Growing Block
    perspective 48
    theory 41, 42

haecceity 142–3
    elements, sharing 142
    resistance/robustness 15
hammer consideration, debate 112
Hammer Problem 111–12
heterogeneous reduction 102
heuristics, impact 79
Higgs boson, discovery 119 n.7
hinge propositions (Wittgenstein)
        146
hippogryph, mental image 130
How the Laws of Physics Lie
        (Cartwright) 92 n.2
human brain, conceptual scheme 33
human conceptual scheme 33
human endowments 34

Hume, David 3
hypostatisation, form 73–4

iambic tetrameter, achievement 82–3
idealisation 111
idealism, forms 109–10
Idealization and the Aims of Science
(Potochnik) 105 n.19
identification
conditions 21–2
enabling 5
identifying knowledge, reference
(function) 29
identity
assertion 80–1
conditions, satisfaction 21–2
copula 67
eliminative effect 80–1
illegimtimate *suggestio falsi*,
conveyance 19
Images of Science (Churchland/
Hooker) 5 n.3
imaginability/conceivability,
distinction (Descartes) 130
imagining, case 138
imperative force 57
imperatives, utterances 14
implicit metaphysical aim 107
implied prescriptive element 74
inapt locution 123
incommensurabilities/
inconsistencies 2
incommensurability,
manifestation 3 n.1
incommensurable subdiscourses
application 33–4
role 37
independence, idea (motivation) 150
individuation conditions 21–2
ineliminable asymmetry 46
inference 65

licensing 65–6
validity, demonstration 70
validity/soundness concepts,
roles 71
inference-licensing 69
inferential frameworks, positions
(occupancy) 45
inflammation, reference 28–9
inflationary theory 34–5
information
conveyance, true propositions
(usage) 66–7
identification 55
informational value 54
ingenuity, paradigm 116–17
'Instrumentalist's New Clothes, The'
(Rowbottom) 92 n.2
intelligibility
transfer 80
underwriting 139
intensional associations 101
intentional concepts,
irreducibility 38
intentional phenomena 80–1
interest-independence 58
internal domain 156–7
Interpretation of Frege's Philosophy,
The (Dummett) 24 n.7
interrogative force 57
interrogatives, utterances 14
intersubstitutivity, ignorance-induced
failure (function) 62
'Is Existence a Predicate?' (Pears)
146 n.4
items, properties/collections
(extension) 52

Kant, Immanuel 3, 122
cognitive neuropsychology,
alignment 33
epistemology 32–3

kinds
  artificial kind sortals,
      determinateness 96
  discourse, question 92
  projected arrangements,
      equivalence 90
  realism, preservation 94–5
kinetic energy, exercise 141–2
knowledge
  achievement 114–15
  application 29
  claims, logical properties 45
  enterprises 115
  identification 49
knowledge-claim 20–1
Kripke, Saul 122
Kukulé (ourobouros dream) 130–1

Lamplight Problem 111–12
language
  artefact 124 n.11
  eternal sentence 61
  games, conception (Wittgenstein)
      153 n.12
  non-trivially uttered sentence 61
  sentences, meaning 46
  term, use 152
laws of thought (Aristotle) 126
learnability constraints 96–7
learning
  assimilation 100
  capability 118
  practice, identification 100
leaving, strategic value 134–5
Leibniz-Clarke Correspondence, The
      (Clarke) 41 n.8
Leiniz, Gottfried Wilheim (relational
      time perspective) 40–1
'likeness' (imputation) 82
linguistic community
  communicative needs/capacities,
      growth 12

use, conformity 154
literal identification, intention
      (absence) 80
literal realism option, doubt 91
literal resemblance 80
Logical Basis of Metaphysics, The
      (Dummett) 150 n.8
logical necessity 122
  absence 121
Logic and Philosophy of Time
      (Blackburn/Hasle/Øhrstrøm)
      44 n.12
Logic of Scientific Discovery, The
      (Popper) 131 n.13
Logico-linguistic Papers
      (Wittgenstein) 146
logics, formal case 31

'making sense'
  epistemic aim, constraint 119–20
  meaning 118–19
Many Faces of Realism, The (Putnam)
      151 n.10
many-valued propositional logics,
      idea 53
mathematical space, point (location)
      41
mathematical structures, reduction
      145
mathematics
  anti-realist perspective 99
  beauty 119
  unreasonable effectiveness 112
matter, microstructure 113
McTaggart argument 42
*Meaning and Necessity: A Study in
      Semantics and Modal Logic*
      (Carnap) 16 n.4
meaning, knowledge 95
meanings
  anti-individualistic accounts 97
  matter, reinvitation 63

publicity/stability 76
public meaning, guarantee
        (securing) 96–7
mechanics, Newtonian theories
        113 n.5
mental models, creation 32
mental phenomena
    physical correlates 103
    property-dualism, implication 38
mental states, content (impact) 93
message
    delivery, request 54–5
    term, usage 48
metaphor
    conceptual metaphor theory 79
    definition 80
    distinction 82–3
    literal identification 83–4
    misdirection, risk 77–8
    nature, conception (clarity) 83–4
    selection 82–3
    understanding 84
    uses, cognitive outcomes 84
metaphorical assertions 78
metaphorical illumination, power
        83–4
*Metaphors and Analogies in Sciences
        and Humanities* (Grayling/
        Wuppuluri) 77 n.1
metaphor, usage 2, 77
    assertion, contrast 79–80
    irreducible use 49
metaphysical conclusions, deferral 86
metaphysical necessity
    concept 126
    imputation 121
metaphysical questions,
        implications 8
metaphysical realism 137–9
    assumption 157
    clue 149
    predication 143

qualification, requirement 139
    rejection, implication 7–8
metaphysical reality, concept 149
    reliance 159
metaphysical realm 138–9
metaphysical thesis 150
metaphysics, discussions 44
metaterm 69–70, 72, 76
    denotation 73–4
methodological forms, reductionism
        (relationship) 104
methodological reduction 104–5
methodological scepticism 110
metonymy 85
    form 86
    understanding 84
metre, choice (poetic significance)
        82–3
Millikan, Robert 116
mind
    cognitive architecture 33
    cognitive processes 78
mind-talk, ontologies (projection) 38
minimalism 59
misdirection 82–3
    risk 77–8
modality 109
    appearance 120
    conditional aspect 135
'Models and Reality' (Putnam)
        152 n.11
models/maps, relation (question) 111
'Model Theory and the Factuality
        of Semantics' (Putnam)
        154 n.14
money terms 68
'mortal-immortal' polarity 124 n.11
multiple interpenetrations 17
multiple realisability
    problem 103
    problems, responses 104
mutatis mutandis 43

mutual contingencies, domain (concept) 124
mutual interpenetrations 17

naïve realism
    conception, Parmenides challenge 4–5
    implicit acceptance 149–50
narrow meaning, broad meaning (distinction) 93
'Native Metaphysics' (Fine/Kit) 11 n
natural grammar 11
natural kinds
    groupings, comparison 89–90
    idea, destabilisation 94
    sortal definitions 96
    terms, usage 93–4
natural language
    grammar, universal categories 1–2
    grammatical features, outline taxonomy 12–13
    sentence, assertoric mode 14
    understanding 1
    words, formation 62 n.3
'Natural Language Metaphysics' (Bach) 11 n
natural language ontology 11
    meaning 11 n
    methodologies 9
    terms 33
natural laws, statements 127
natural move, usage 23
Natural Ontological Attitude, Fine invocation 5–6
"Natural Ontological Attitude, The" (Fine) 5 n.4
natural ontological case, pretheoretical meanings 6
nature, idealisation/phenomena 105
'necessary being'
    idea, questioning 126
    solution, arbitrariness 124–5

'necessary existence' (conception) 125
neurogenesis, analysis 116–17
neurological events, reduction 101
neurology, discourse (reduction) 86
'Neurophilosophical Approach to Perception' (Gouvela/Northoff) 33 n.2
Neurophilosophy (Churchland) 102 n.13, 155 n.15
neuropsychology
    anticipators 32–3
    pessimism, sharing (question) 133
Newtonian concept, Clarke defense 40–1
Nichomachean Ethics (Aristotle) 25
nominal essences, real essences (distinction) 25
nominalistic account 62–3
non-divine necessary existence 126
nongeneric univocal meaning 70
non-uniqueness, acceptance 155
nuclear theory, terms (conveniences) 148 n.6

objectivity, Fregean view 95–6
observables (proximal phenomena), inference 90–1
observer effect 112
offered propositions 67
oil drop experiment 116–17
On Certainty (Wittgenstein) 144 n.3, 146
On Duties (Cicero) 62
'On the Character of Philosophic Problems' (Carnap) 101 n.11
ontological anxiety 4
ontological considerations, base case 126–7
ontological forms, reductionism (relationship) 104
ontological reduction 104–5

ontological terminus 125
ontology (ontologies) 11
  basal ontology 1, 36
  discourse projection 20, 159
  grammatical ontology 89
  postulation 35
  projection 1–2, 67, 151–2
ontology-projection 142
'On What There Is' (Quine) 16 n.4
'Open Future, Supervaluationism and
    the Growing-Block Theory:
    A Stage-Theoretical Account'
    (Loss) 41 n.9
opinion, divergence 102
optative force 57
'order of successions' 41
ordinary discourse, imprecisions 50
ordinary language
  logic, presence 19
  usage 20
ourobouros dream 130–1
*Oxford Handbook of the Philosophy of
    Time, The* (Callender) 44 n.12

pain, metaphoric talk 86
paraconsistent descriptions 155
paraconsistent statements, truth
    31 n.1
paraconsistent, term (usage) 31
'Paradox of the Heap, The' (Kamp)
    57 n.18
Parmenides 3, 6
  cognitive neuropsychology,
    alignment 33
  naïve realism challenge 4–5
Parmenides (Plato) 144 n.1
past-tensed statements 46
pattern-seeking 78
Peirce, Charles 158
penetrative recognitional
    capacities 94

perceivers, cognitive activities 31–2
perceiving (action) 155
perceptual discourse
  pretheoretically-assumed primacy
    157–8
  realism, debate 147
perceptual domain, context 121
perceptual environment
  conceptual scheme 31–2
  mental models, creation 32
  reference, concept 25
  thoughts, merits 25
perceptual experience 2–3
  appearance, explanation 140
  conceptual scheme 33–4, 121
  conceptual scheme, ad hoc nature
    33–4
  discourse, understanding 98–9
  environment, discussion 49
  environments, entities/events
    (discussion) 20
  epistemology 144
  ontology 37
  ranges 12
  virtual reality, equivalence 32
perceptual experience domain 138
  actuals, realism 149–50
  considerations 159–60
  restriction, lifting 121
perpetual experience 12
personal attitude, venting 72–3
petitio principii 135
phenomena
  control 114
  existence 35
  reduction 80–1
  referral 105
phenomenal reality, recognition 32–3
phenomena-organising activity 90
philosophical difficulty, source
    (disappearance) 16

Philosophical Investigations
(Wittgenstein) 19 n.5, 68 n.7
philosophical perplexities
host, generation 18
occurrence, restatement 76
philosophical scrutiny 117
Philosophy and the Mirror of Nature
(Rorty) 150 n.7
Philosophy of Language (Dummett)
7 n.5
'Philosophy of Language and Mind'
(Burge) 97 n.9
*Philosophy of Quantum Mechanics,
The* (Jammer) 5 n.2
philosophy of science
anti-realist views 91
realist-anti-realism debate
91–2
phlegmasia (medical term) 28–9
phrastics
expressibility 14
impact 61
physical environment, sensitivity
(degree) 48
physical events 18
physicalism 103
physical particulars 18, 120–1
physical phenomena
property-dualism, implication 38
structure/properties, scientific
investigation 36
physics, law (nomological
necessity) 126
pinhole
metaphor 110–11
problem 118
place-holder
duty, execution 26
role 26
Planck length, examination 34–5
Plato 3, 110

cognitive neuropsychology,
alignment 33
point-instant, idealisation 48
point, sense 53
polar concept argument 110
polar-concept consideration 125–6
positive epistemic
evaluation 70
evaluation, predicate 64
predicate 64–5
value 76
possibility/conceivability
distinction, maintenance 129
notions, conflation 128
possible-worlds, representation 46
postmodernism 9
practical possibility/conditional
necessity, concepts
(interaction) 121
pragmatic motivation 91
pragmatics 2
precisifications 51, 53–4
attainment 50
dispensing 54
presence 55
technical precisification 51
predecessor, role 28
predicates
providing 27
shorthand 26–7
predicating (action) 155
predicating truth 65
predication 26–7, 64
grammatical form 13–14
'is' statement 81
truth-conditions,
supervaluational/
subvaluational theories 52
predicative form 61
predictions, generation 65
prepositions, development 12

presupposition, fulfilment
    (requirement) 43
pretend-assertion 73
pretended assertion 75–6
pretheoretical intuition 24 n.7
pretheoretically-assumed primacy
    157–8
primitive referring expressions,
    definition 12
Principle of Sufficient Reason 125
problematic scepticism 109
projected arrangements, kinds
    (equivalence) 90
projectivist model 67
property
    imputation, example 81
    predication, treatment 54
    semantic indeterminacy,
      equivalence 56–7
property-dualism, implication 38
property-emergence, admission 18
propositions 60
    disvalued propositions 66
    duality 66–7
    epistemic necessity 122
    expression 63
    offered propositions 67
    statement/theory, predication
      26–7
    substantive properties 76
prosententialism 59
proximal phenomena (observables),
    inference 90–1
pseudoscience 119
psychological contents, reduction 101
psychological discourses
    domain 141
    inclusion 18
psychology
    discourse 145
    intentional phenomena 80–1

'Publicity, Stability and "Knowing the
    Meaning"' (Grayling) 56 n.17,
    76 n.13, 97 n.8
public meaning, guarantee (securing)
    96–7
public policy formulation 117

quantitative methodologies 117
quantum field, theory 148
quantum phenomena 85
quantum states, superposition
    (explanation) 83
quantum theory 79
    concept, impact 2–3
    Copenhagen interpretations 112
    experimental set-up, usage 112
    ontology, Einstein/Bohr debate 5
quasi-Wittgensteinian view,
    involvement 157
question-begging 71–2
questions, postponement 148

'Radical Physicalism and the "Real
    World"' (Neurath) 101 n.11
radical translation, opacity
    (reduction) 62
Railway Clearing House, GMT
    adoption 40
rational respect 75
Readings in Philosophical Analysis
    (Feigl/Sellars) 69 n.8
real, concept (collapse) 17
'real' definition 15
real essences
    doctrine, revival 90
    nominal essences, distinction 25
realism
    acceptance 146
    commitment 100
    deferral 146
    definition 139–40

derivation, naïve realism
    (impact) 99
    distinction 137
    literal approach 135
    metaphysical realism 137
    relation 143
realism-anti-realism debate 91–2
'Realism, Antirealism, Irrealism,
    Quasi-Realism' (Wright)
    71 n.9
realism-anti-realism opposition 7
Realism with a Human Face
    (Putnam) 150 n.8
realist assumption, power 140–1
reality 137
    denial, impossibility 6–7
    description 154–5
    question 160
    touchstone, shift 6
'Reality Without Reference', '
    A Coherence Theory of
    Truth and Knowledge'
    (Davidson) 59 n.1
realm of fact, inconceivability 134
real reality, identification (problem) 4
'real things' 140
real world, identification
    (question) 123
reasoning
    needs 126
    parity 133
recognition 78
recognitional capacities 27–8, 95
    acquisition 153–4
    speaker need 25
red, hues 49
reduced/reducing classes,
    intersubstitution 81
reducible domain
    realism, relation 143
    realistic attitude 145–6

reducing discourse, usage 102
reduction 89
    account, demand 18
    account, making 106
    aim 106–7
    attempts 31 n.1
    concept 106
    epistemic reduction 104–5
    heterogeneous reduction 102
    incompleteness 106
    meaning 100–1
    methodological reduction 104–5
    ontological reduction 104–5
    revisionary status 103
    translation, usage (distinctions)
    101
reductionisms, taxonomisation 104
redundancy 59
reference
    concept 25
    concept, equivocation 157–8
    considerations 28
    description theory 94–5
    descriptive knowledge,
    relationship 22
    discourse-relativity 26
    fixed sense, absence 152
    function 29
    grammatical form 13–14
    success 23–4
    theories 21
    theory of reference, choice
    (determination) 67
    time 44
    understanding 21
'Reference and Modality'
    (Quine) 94 n.5
referential access (derailment),
    falsehood (impact) 24
referential-attributive distinction
    23–4

referential connections,
    establishment 23–4
referents
    actuality, commitment 11 n
    assertion 20–1
    assertion, truth-values 28
    constellation, equivalence 24
    discourse 140
    discoursers 140
    domain-dependently conception
        153
    identification 29
    knowledge-claim 20–1
    ontology 140
    perceptual acquaintance 25
    total ontology 140
referring (action) 155
referring expression, use 14
referring terms
    connection, intimacy 21
    rigid designators 22
Refutation of Scepticism, The
    (Grayling) 124, n.11
regress, chain 124–5
relational predicate, case collections
    27–8
relations, matrix 123–4
relative polarities 126–7
relativistic irrealism 75–6
religious discourse, domain 159–60
remembering (intentional
    phenomena) 80–1
representation
    coverage 156
    epistemological innocence,
        absence 154
    idea 150–1
Representation and Reality (Putnam)
    150 n.8, 154 n.13
representing (action) 155
rhetorical device, choice 83

rigidity, predication 67
risks/benefits, balance (clarity) 116
Roche, Boyle 63 n.5
Roger Bacon on Signs (Maloney)
    13 n.2
Russellian view 14, 15

salience, meriting 106
salva veritate 81
sayings, class 73
sayings-that, subset 73
sceptical considerations,
    problems 110
scepticism 109
    methodological scepticism 110
    reason 131
Schrodinger's cat, analogy 118–19
science, common language 101
scientific anti-realism, formal
    defence 92
scientific discourse
    domains 36–7
    realism, debate 147
    reduction 3
Scientific Image, The (van Fraasen)
    5 n.3
scientific realism, predication 92
seeing-as 103
self-subsistent unitary entities 147–8
semantic anti-realism, interpretation
    (identification) 7–8
semantic assignment (process),
        substitution (usage) 84
semantic indeterminacy 55–6
    occurrence 56
    property, equivalence 56–7
semantic machinery, assimilation 156
Sense and Sensibility (Austen) 19 n.5
sense-force-point 53
sense-making 78
    assumption 157

enterprise 118–19
    function 146
sense, paraconsistency 151
sensory equipment 34–5
sentences
    meaning 46
    non-trivial utterances 62
sentential contexts, predicate
        (providing) 27
sentient beings, welfare 28
Sextus Empiricus 109
shared assumptions 122
shoes
    necessity 120–1
    search 120
shorthand, usage 73–4
Sigma 5 evaluation 119
simile
    analogy, contrast 81–2
    role 77
    uses, cognitive outcomes 84
slippage, potential 84
social domain, actuality
        (achievement) 143
social experience, domain 140, 142
social science enquiry 117
sortal definitions 96
soundness, concepts (roles) 71
space, conceptions (connection) 47
spatial metaphor, irreducibility 48
spatial occupancy, idea 47–8
spatio-temporal domain 140
spatio-temporally conditioned
        intuitions, organisation
        32–3
spatio-temporal material
        particulars 120
spatio-temporal realm, existence/
        character 20–1
spatio-temporal world 158

speakers
    epistemic capacities 95
    idiolects 94
specialist vocabularies, construction 51
specious present, idea 41
speech time 44
Spinoza, Baruch 3
stability 66
Standard Model, atomic theory
        147–8
standing statements 61–2
statement of conditional
        necessity 127
statements of natural laws 127
state of affairs, contingency 127
states of affairs, assertions 72
stereotype-conception view 96
stereotypes, usage 94, 96
straddling effect 91
string theory 148
    claims, empirical tests 119
sub-concepts 34
subject, interference 112
Subjective View, The (McGinn)
        132 n.14
subject-matter, assimilation 14
substantive properties 63–4
substantive truth, theories 59–60
substitution, usage 84
subvaluational/dialetheist
        approach 53
successor, role 28
supernatural powers 142
superposed quantum states 82
superposition 2
supervaluational/subvaluational
        theories 52
supervenience 103
Suszko Reduction 53
Syene, shadows (absence) 116

'Systematically Misleading
    Expressions' (Ryle) 144
systematic epistemological
    considerations 140

target, property/component 79–80
taxonomic theory, evolution 90
taxonomies, differences (result)
    17–18
taxonomisation 17
technical concepts 1
technical prececisification 51
teleological considerations,
    invocation 106
telescopy, usage 113
temporal concepts
    deployment, spatial metaphor
        (irreducibility) 48
    function 42
temporal logic, discussions 44
temporal phenomena, philosophical
    attention 41
temporal reference, involvement 45
terms
    meaning (knowing), constraint
        (ignoring) 94
    meaning, unknowability 96–7
    metadata 69–70
    semantics, expected property 57
    truth-values 52
testability, prospects 119–20
test-case presupposition 4–5
Theaetetus, question 109
theory of inflation 119 n.8
theory of reference, choice
    (determination) 67
Thinking Fast and Slow (Kahneman)
    114 n.6
thought
    electro-chemical activity 38

independence 158
judgment, involvement 68 n.7
remainderless reduction, question
    37–8
thought-experiment 93
thought-game, impact 35
time
    application 47–8
    conceptions, connection 47
    empty container, perspective
        40–1
    existence, simultaneity 41
    explicit measures, significance 47
    reminders, assemblage 39–40
    subjectively different lengths,
        coordination 39–40
    univocal concept 41–2
    unreality, demonstration 46–7
    unreality, establishment 42
timeline, visualization 48
time-relations 46–7
toolkit metaphor, usage 46–7
tout court 28, 128, 134
    domain 138
Tractatus Logico-Philosophicus
    (Wittgenstein) 13
transcendental arguments, logic 127
transitivity 2 n.1
translation, usage 102
truth
    approaches 59
    assertion, interdependence 73
    assertion, relationship 59
    considerations 28
    degrees, speaker acceptance 52–3
    discourse-relativity 76
    discussion 69
    grounds for truth (Frege
        distinction) 154–5
    importance, challenge 60

independently-specified
concept 71
metaterm perspective, failure
(artefact) 76
minimalist theories 27
a posteriori discovery 122
Pragmatists's theory 113
pragmatist theory 66
predicating 65
substantive property 59–60
substantive property, relation
63–4
theory 68
theory (Davidson) 27 n.8
tout court 21
'Truth and Indefinability' (Grayling)
27 n.8, 100 n.10
Truth and Other Enigmas (Dummett)
150 n.8
Truth and Truthfulness (Williams)
74 n.11
truth-bearers 60
examples 61
substantive property 21, 27
truth, concept 71
discourse-relativity, application 26
temptation, undermining 156
truth-condition
recognition-transcendence 56
supervaluational/subvaluational
theories 52
work 42–3
truth-evaluable utterances,
appropriateness 57
truth-for-that-domain, concept 68–9
'Truth' in *Logico- Linguistic Papers*
(Strawson/Strawon) 71 n.10
truth-values 29, 56
A-property-predicating statement
possession, requirement 43
assignment, just-current ground
45–6

future-tensed statements,
truth-value 44
gaps, extension 56–7
gaps, supervaluation 53
possibility (Łukasiewicz
suggestion) 53
postulation 52–3
a priori determination 122
referent-dependence 28
switch 54
van Fraasen discussion 5
'Twin Earth' discussion 93
'Types, Rigidity and A Posteriori
Necessity' (Collins) 94 n.5

'Über Sinn und Bedeutung' (Frege)
24 n.7
ultimate reality
concept 1, 160–1
constitution 6–7
Cretan Paradox-like ascription
160–1
location, tendentious place 35
relation 135
uncertainty 2
'Undecidability of the Spectral Gap'
(Cubitt et al.) 3 n.1
uniqueness 154–5
universal whiteness 144
universe
forward history, bifurcation 83
human perspective, point of
origin 36
univocal conception, availability
(absence) 42
'Unreality of Time, The' (McTaggart)
42 n.10
unreasonable effectiveness 112
'Unreasonable Effectiveness of
Mathematics in the Natural
Sciences, The' (Wigner) 1112
usefulness 52

utility
  desiderata, fulfillment 66
  relationship 65–6
utterances
  circumstances 67
  discourse-relative content 71
  phrastics 61
  truth-evaluable components 61
'Utterer's Meaning and Intentions'
    (Grice) 97 n.7

vague expressions, usefulness 55–6
vagueness
  Locke philosophy 58
  subvaluational approaches,
    consequence 56
validity, concepts (roles) 71
van Fraasen, Bas (truth-values
    discussion) 5
Venn diagrams, blur 17
Verne, Jules (fictions) 130
View From Nowhere, The (Nagel)
    132 n.14
virtual entities, domain 90

virtual reality 3–4
  constituents 33
  perceptual experience,
    equivalence 32
visual field, blind spot (filling-in) 32

water, behaviour/facts 28
wave-particle duality 2
whiteness, instantiation 143–4
Williams, Bernard 74
'Will String Theory Finally be Put
    to the Experimental Test?'
    (Foster) 119 n.8
witches, belief 142
Wittgenstein, Ludwig 19
  debate 153–4
Words and Life (Putnam) 150 n.8
world
  patchwork view, acceptance
    159–60
  term, use 152
world-perception relation,
    epistemological aspect
    150–1